CONTEMPORARY GREAT LAKES
POW WOW REGALIA

CONTEMPORARY GREAT LAKES POW WOW REGALIA

"*Nda Maamawigaami* (Together We Dance)"

Edited by Marsha MacDowell

Photographs by Minnie Wabanimkee

Michigan State University Museum
East Lansing, Michigan

Nokomis Learning Center
Okemos, Michigan

Left: Tony Chingwa (center). Hastings Pow Wow, 1968. Photo courtesy of Charlton Park and Historical Village Museum.

The terms Odawa, Ottawa, Ojibwe, Chippewa, Ojibwa, and Ojibway have had different cultural and political meanings throughout history. This project has attempted to honor individual artist preference for tribal affiliation and spelling.

On the cover:
Calvin Littlehill (Navajo), Wyoming, Michigan. Annual Homecoming of the Three Fires, Grand Rapids, Michigan, 1996.

CONTENTS

ACKNOWLEDGMENTS

"Contemporary Great Lakes Pow Wow Regalia: *Nda Maamawigaami* (Together We Dance)" is a collaborative activity of the Nokomis Learning Center and the Michigan Traditional Arts Program of the Michigan State University Museum. It was made possible by the financial and in-kind support of the Ruth Mott Fund, the Michigan Council for Arts and Cultural Affairs, the Miller Brewing Company, the Saginaw-Chippewa Indian Tribe of Mt. Pleasant, the MSU Office of the Provost, and the Lila Wallace-Reader's Digest Community Folklife Program administered by The Fund for Folk Culture and underwritten by the Lila Wallace-Reader's Digest Fund.

Thanks to the artists and dancers who contributed their time and skills to this project: Thurman Bear, Jason George, Catherine Gibson, Tony Miron, Elizabeth Osawamick, Judy Pierzynowski, Stanley Peltier, Dennis Shananaquet, Bedahbin Webkamigad, Rochelle Shano Whitepigeon, and Linda Topash Yazel. The project benefitted greatly from the counsel of knowledgeable elders and cultural leaders: Thurman Bear, George Cornell, Anna Crampton, Deborah Galvan, Arnie Parish, Kenny Pheasant, Helen Roy, and Kathryn VanDeCar.

Special recognition is due Sally Thielen, who created the ceramic masks for the display mannequins. Marclay Crampton, Tony Miron, Stoney Polman, Dennis Shananaquet, Kelsey Wabanimkee, and Theresa Weller allowed their faces to be cast during the creation of the masks. Marclay Crampton crafted the small art objects that adorn the limited edition version of the exhibition catalogue. Minnie Wabanimkee served as project photographer. Historical photographs were graciously loaned by Frank Ettawageshik, Charlton Park and Historical Village Museum, and Esther Koon.

Without the support and involvement of the following individuals, the exhibition and its catalogue would not have been possible: Frances Vincent, exhibit designer, MSU Museum; Melanie Atkinson, Michele Beltran, Kristin Corra, LaNeysa Harris-Featherstone, Lynne Swanson, and Pearl Wong, collection management staff, MSU Museum; Erica Adams, program assistant, MSU Museum; Francie Freese, transcriber, MSU Museum; Marclay Crampton, fieldworker, Nokomis Learning Center; Kristan Tetens, publication editor and project manager, University Relations; Cynthia Lounsbery, publication design manager, University Relations; Kathryn Darnell, illustrator; and Judy DeJaegher, Terry Hanson, Noé Hernandez, and Ruth Patino, MSU Museum administrative support staff.

Special thanks are also extended to the Nokomis Learning Center Board of Directors, the MSU Museum Associates Board of Directors, the MSU Museum Development Council, and these individuals who provided support and guidance through the fundraising process: Peter Mattir, Sarah Warner, Casey Granton, and Deborah Tuck.

We would like to recognize the dancers and elders in each of the communities for their support of this project. Various pow wow committees graciously permitted us to photograph their gatherings. Finally, a special thanks to the families and friends of the artists, who helped in many ways. To all of them, we say *Megwetch*.

Cameron Wood   Marsha MacDowell
Nokomis Learning Center   Michigan State University Museum

Left: Fred Ettawageshik by Virgil D. Haynes of Harbor Springs, Michigan. Photo courtesy of Frank Ettawageshik.

Above: Veteran Cherokee dancer Don Manies of Muskegon carries an eagle staff in memory of T. Shalifoe. Morning Star Traditional Pow Wow, Muskegon, 1996.

Below: Fancy Dancer. Michigan State University American Indian Heritage Pow Wow, East Lansing, 1995.

INTRODUCTION

MARSHA MACDOWELL AND CAMERON WOOD

Pow wows are important social and cultural gatherings for Native Americans living in the Great Lakes region; they are also occasions where the elaborate creations of many individuals play an important role in the maintenance of artistic traditions. Music and dance are an integral part of these gatherings; equally important is the regalia, or dance apparel, worn by participants.* Certain dances require particular types of regalia. Included in a set of regalia for a dance may be bustles, head pieces, dresses, shirts, leggings, footwear, sashes, shawls, and hand-held items such as fans or purses. The various components may be made by the dancer, a relative, or friend, or obtained through purchase or trade at pow wows. Within families or communities, regalia makers are usually known for their outstanding work in one medium, such as beadwork or leatherwork.

From left to right: Carli Shananaquet, Lorraine Shananaquet, Shannon Martin, and Julie Block. Michigan State University American Indian Heritage Pow Wow, East Lansing, 1995.

Although this apparel reflects the artistic skill and knowledge of many individuals, little attention has been paid to regalia artists beyond the Native American community. "Contemporary Great Lakes Pow Wow Regalia: *Nda Maamawigaami* (Together We Dance)," is a multi-faceted collaborative project of the Michigan State University Museum and the Nokomis Learning Center designed to document and showcase the work of contemporary American Indian regalia artists. By bringing this kind of artistry to an audience well beyond those who participate in pow wows, we hope that the awareness of and appreciation for this vital, culturally based art will be greatly broadened.

Both Native and non-Native Americans have been involved in all phases of the development and implementation of this project. The project has been especially blessed by the wise counsel and input of Native Americans with vast and respected experience in pow wows. Their guidance was critical in the drafting of questions to ask dancers and artists, the identification of interview subjects, and the review and improvement of the exhibition's labels and catalogue.

---

*The term "regalia" is used widely in the Great Lakes region, although other terms are used to describe the special attire worn by dancers and other important people at tribal and inter-tribal events. In a recent article on Lakota pow wows, William K. Powers prefers the word "costume" to describe "ceremonial dress, dress clothing, outfit, regalia, Indian clothes, (even) chief suit and other terms. . . . In English, [the word] costume, when used generically, refers to an ensemble of outer clothing worn by women and men reflective of a particular period or time, country, class, or event. In its more powerful usage, costume is something that enhances, or adds, to everyday clothing" ("Innovation in Lakota Pow Wow Costumes," *American Indian Art Magazine*, Autumn 1994, p. 67).

From the outset, it was the goal of the project coordinators to feature the "voices" of Native artists and dancers. Thus, one of the primary tasks of the project was to identify individuals who could represent the artistry and experience of scores of contemporary dancers and regalia makers in the Great Lakes area. Eventually, Nokomis Learning Center staff members selected Thurman Bear, Jason George, Catherine Gibson, Tony Miron, Elizabeth Osawamick, Judy Pierzynowski, Stanley Peltier, Dennis Shananaquet, Bedahbin Webkamigad, Rochelle Shano Whitepigeon, and Linda Topash Yazel.

These artists and their work were documented through tape-recorded interviews with Marclay Crampton and in stunning color photography by Minnie Wabanimkee. One set of regalia for each of the six major dance styles (Men's Traditional, Women's Traditional, Jingle, Fancy Shawl, Grass, and Fancy) was obtained by purchase or commission. The interviews, photographs, and regalia collection became the basis of the exhibition. A series of masks cast from the faces of dancers by artist Sally Thielen are used on the mannequins displaying the regalia. After the exhibition has ended, these materials will be housed at the Michigan State University Museum, where they will be accessible for future study, exhibits, and educational programs.

Top: Tom Showmin (right) and an unidentified dancer. Day of the Eagle Pow Wow, East Jordan, 1996.

Bottom: Men socializing. Sault Ste. Marie Tribal National Assembly, 14th Annual Traditional Pow Wow and Spiritual Conference, 1996.

In addition to the permanent collection of research materials and dance regalia produced in the course of creating this exhibition, this catalogue provides another lasting record of a unique artistic heritage. Illustrated with historical photographs from family archives and with photographic portraits by Minnie Wabanimkee, it includes essays on the role of dance and regalia in contemporary Native American life, the history and meaning of pow wows in Michigan, and the dances and dance regalia that are common to the state. It also features descriptions of the six dances featured in the exhibit

and a glossary of terms associated with materials and techniques used in making regalia.

When a Native American acquaintance heard that one of the goals of the exhibit was to display the artistic merit of pow wow dance regalia, he responded: "Well, you know, it's the dancer's moves and attitude that really matter." His comment underscores the fundamental relationship between the art of regalia and dance, and between art and cultural meaning.

Dance regalia was never meant to be placed on display in exhibit galleries. It was meant to be worn by dancers, and its artistic merit can be truly judged only in the context of dancing. Through the "Contemporary Great Lakes Pow Wow Regalia: *Nda Maamawigaami* (Together We Dance)" project, we hope that individuals will not only become more aware of this art form, but also that they gain an appreciation of its importance in the perpetuation of traditional dancing in native communities. Once visitors have seen the artistry on display in this exhibit, we challenge them to attend a pow wow, listen to the drum, watch the dancers, witness the judging. Here, in its natural context, is where you will be best able to understand and appreciate the skills and talents of dancers and regalia makers.

Top: Traditional Dancers. Morning Star Traditional Pow Wow, Muskegon, 1996.

Bottom: JoAnn Whitehouse and Keith Cameron. Michigan State University American Indian Heritage Pow Wow, East Lansing, 1996.

3

NATIVE AMERICAN DANCE: CEREMONIES AND SOCIAL TRADITIONS

CHARLOTTE HETH

American Indian dance exists everywhere in America and in every possible venue, from the most traditional and private spaces to those most public and accessible.[1] Thousands of dancers perform every day in out-of-the way places—not to satisfy paying audiences, but to ensure the continuation of longstanding lifeways, to honor deities and each other, to associate with friends and kin, and to affirm their Indian identities. Others showcase Native American dance on the stage, sometimes incorporating ballet, modern dance, or abridged versions of traditional dances.

Most Indian dances are non-commercial and succeed with nothing but word-of-mouth advertising; some charge admission and are advertised through flyers or notices in newspapers. Most dances neither cultivate nor expect an audience from outside their community; some seek audiences to help support the event economically as well as to share in other educational, social, and cultural activities.

The best performers and leaders (or choreographers) rely on time-tested notions of space, time, music, dress, adornment, and steps to create dance events. Most dancers learn by participating from childhood and dancing throughout their lives. A few enroll in classes, take private or group lessons, or complete apprenticeships with master Indian dancers. Most make their own dance apparel or commission it from friends and family. Few make any money practicing their art.

Although many dances and ceremonies are performed regularly by Indians living on or near reservations or in rural areas of the United States and Canada, new contexts—like urban Indian gatherings and pow wows—foster the composition, change, and continuation of certain traditions. Music and dance are frequently shared across tribal boundaries in an ever-expanding circle of tradition. Whether the songs and dances came originally from the Creator, another deity, a guardian spirit, a slain monster, or even an animal, human choreographers and composers have always played the most important part in creating and perpetuating Native American music and dance.

After European contact, many Indians were dispersed from aboriginal lands to new homelands, cities, or reservations as a result of wars, inducements by treaty, and other economic and political forces. While some peoples disappeared altogether, some smaller groups intermarried with neighboring peoples, both Indian and non-Indian, or were adopted by larger tribes. Government agents often grouped peoples together arbitrarily or because of language and cultural similarities or geographical proximity. This widespread destruction and dislocation of tribes and their cultures profoundly affected Indian music and dance.

A longer version of this article originally appeared in Native American Dance: Ceremonies and Social Traditions *(Smithsonian Institution National Museum of the American Indian and Starwood/Fulcrum Publishing, Inc., 1992). The excerpt is reprinted here with the permission of the publisher and the author.*

Indian religious practices, the nexus for most dances, were often banned by churches and colonial governments. When the Pueblo Indians of New Mexico and Arizona revolted in 1680 and forced the Spanish south to El Paso, they gained concessions regarding taxation and governance and the moderation of European religious persecution. After the revolt, native religions and dances were practiced, to some extent, alongside Catholic rituals. While the United States government's ban on Indian religions in the nineteenth century targeted the Sun Dance and Ghost Dance in particular, it affected all other native religions as well. In Canada, the government seized many beautiful ceremonial objects and much dance regalia when Northwest Coast Indian potlatches became illegal.[2] In the twentieth century, economic necessity and a federal relocation program have compelled many Indians to migrate to cities. Their creative solution for surviving urban alienation has been to start pow wow clubs with other Indian community members. Plains Indian music and dance dominate these clubs, regardless of the multiplicity of their members' heritages.

Dance still occupies an important position within many Indian groups that continue to practice the old religions and dances vital to their way of life. Because so many dances and songs have spiritual and supernatural sources, they retain their original significance and value. These traditional dances, often tied to seasonal or life-cycle events, are regionally or tribally specific; the singers usually perform in native languages, and the ceremonies unfold according to ancient calendars and belief systems. Some are public dances; others are private or semi-public. They include dances for curing, prayer, initiation, storytelling, performing magic, playing games, courting, hunting, and influencing nature. In performing these songs, dances, and rituals, the Indians of today reaffirm their ties to a living culture.

Most traditional dances do not offer complete individual freedom of expression. Rather, each dancer expresses himself or herself in physical action within the bounds of traditional dance forms. Dance forms vary because Native Americans are different not only from other peoples but from each other as well. Some dance forms are solos, many are ensembles. Many of the latter have a leader and a chorus; some are unison groups; others are groups with featured soloists. A few forms emphasize the dancer's individualistic style; others are multi-part dances, with the dancers occupying a variety of roles.

Almost always, Native American dance is accompanied by music. In some parts of North America, rattles are the most popular instrument. In other regions, the drum predominates. Decorative elements on the outfits worn by dancers provide additional sounds: adornments of bone, shells, and metallic cones or jingles are percussive and melodic sounds integral to the dance. The beat of feet against the ground adds another dimension of sound.

Some Indian dances are very acrobatic and demand great physical skill, strength, and agility. Others are very restrained, with the dancers taking small steps and staying close to the earth. These also demand strength and endurance because the dancer may have to dance for long periods of time (sometimes all day or night) or maintain certain body positions. Some expressions in dance require crouching or bent-over postures, in which the dancer stays for an entire musical phrase or longer section of the dance. Some dancers mimic animals and birds; others the work of hunting, fishing, harvesting and preparing food, other occupations, or warfare.

The largest motions are often in the torso and head, with very few twists of the dancer's body. When they are extended, the feet act as a unit with the legs, and the hands with the arms. Small movements of the forearms and wrists occur when the dancer shakes an implement such as a rattle, stick, or branch. Customarily, Indian dances require communal interaction, cooperation, compliance with group norms, and—not accidentally—several generations of participants.

The dance space is often conceived of in terms of circles, with the dancers moving clockwise or counterclockwise as determined by their cosmology and worldview. Other dance orientations involve line dancers moving forward or backward in unison or dancing in place, and dancers moving in a processional into and out of larger dance areas.

The directions of the dances, the words to the music, the number of repetitions, the choice and manufacture of instruments, the dress and bodily adornment, and the interaction of the performers are often symbolic in nature and cannot be properly observed without knowing something about native belief systems. Indeed, in Indian life, the dance is not possible without the belief systems and the music, and the belief systems and the music hardly exist without the dance.

On the whole, Indian music in North America is vocal and monophonic with rattle and/or drum accompaniment. While many singers use a drum to set the beat and to signal repetitions and changes in dance movements, rattles are the most widespread instrument. Many songs have a wide range, testing the stamina and artistry of the singers. Although most songs are performed in native languages, some include vocables (non-translatable syllables) used to carry the melody in the same way as "fa-la-la" and other vocables do in European folk songs. These vocables are fixed and constitute the "words" to the songs. Variations in vocal style identify tribal and regional differences and genres of songs.

Unlike the elements of most Euro-American classical and folk dance, the elements of American Indian dance are often not predictable: the exact length of a dance, the number of beats before a turn, the number of dancers required, the exact time of the performance, or even whether a rehearsal will be held can vary from event to event. Although many Indian communities offer songs and dances from ancient times, even some of these old ceremonies require new compositions each season. While the ancient standards and beliefs are upheld, new words and tunes appear within the framework, and the dancers must rehearse anew with the singers.

Because Indians in the twentieth century live differently from their ancestors, occasions for the performance of music and dance have expanded to non-traditional settings. In the 1990s, Indian singers and dancers can be found at Indian and county fairs, public receptions honoring Indian and other dignitaries, national Indian conferences, political rallies, crafts fairs, public programs of museums and colleges, demonstrations by Indian political activists, graduation ceremonies, tourist attractions, amusement parks, and in various Indian education programs.

Experienced dancers who exhibit excellence and expertise are acknowledged in their communities as lead or head dancers or as teachers. Sometimes excellence is recognized through blanket dances or honoring ceremonies such as giveaways. Mastery and artistry are also rewarded at competitive dances at some pow wows with cash and other prizes.

Some Native American dancers and musicians have become full or part-time professional teachers and performers. Some are retired and wish to share their knowledge and culture; some believe they have a duty to educate the general public and to help abolish negative stereotypes; others teach children to carry on their traditions. Customarily these singers and dancers make extra money by consulting and performing in public. In these contexts, the leaders are usually very careful to maintain the proper presentation of songs and dances, to perform only the more secular selections from their repertoires, and to explain the original context of each dance. The American Indian Dance Theater, the most visible professional troupe, asks formal permission of tribal elders and governments before adapting native dances for the stage. In its extensive program notes, the troupe strives to educate while presenting a visual and aural feast for spectators.

Literacy is a tool that mitigates against change—except, it seems, in Indian dance. Written documentation of Indian dance has been limited, partially due to the constraints of dance notation, which is still evolving. With the advent of video documentation, dancers can now study past performances both for scholarly and performance purposes. When these captured dances are re-created, they will probably be varied to suit the voices and styles of today's singers and dancers. Every day, new dances and genres are composed with new words, melodies, steps, and dress. The contemporary revival of many Indian dances has also fostered a healthy controversy over the authenticity of versions, proper instrumentation and dress, suitable venues, and the ownership of songs, dances, and ceremonies. Some have even questioned whether the old dances should be revived. In the end, however, the dynamics of change—stressing an appreciation of the creative process—and the dynamics of tradition are not antithetical but complementary.

The value of this music and dance to the peoples who created them and still use them cannot be overestimated. Indian music and dance pervade all aspects of life, from creation stories to death and the remembrance of death. The importance of American Indian dance is found not only in its impact on modern society, but also in the traditions and values it expresses to and for the Indian people. This oral tradition has survived solely because the music and dance are too important to be allowed to die. Native peoples' relationships to their creators, their fellow humans, and to nature are what American Indian dance really celebrates.

Notes

[1] The word "traditional," as used by many Indian people and scholars, can be an overarching term with varying meaning. Sometimes it refers to the oldest norms: languages, religions, artistic forms, everyday customs, and individual behaviors. At other times it refers to modern practices based on those norms. Again, it may refer to a time before technological advances. It may even refer to categories of dance, music, and dress that draw most closely on ancient, established practices. Here I am referring to accepted and accustomed places of performance in reservations or rural communities—"dance places."

[2] Potlatches are a form of "giveaway," a ceremony in which the material wealth of a clan or family is shared with those they wish to honor.

Pow Wows in Michigan

Marsha MacDowell and Arnie Parish

A pow wow occurs somewhere in the United States nearly every weekend. Reservations are the most common venue, but city parks, college campuses, basketball and hockey arenas, museums, fairgrounds, shopping malls, and a wide variety of other settings are used by Native Americans who have migrated into urban areas. Some families follow the "Pow Wow Highway" and participate in an event every weekend; others travel only to pow wows close to home.

Derived from traditional seasonal gatherings held by almost all tribes for their friends and allies, the pow wow has emerged as a pan-Indian social event that brings families together to share native traditions. Today, pow wows serve many purposes. Spiritually, pow wows provide a communal occasion for Indian people to celebrate life and to give thanks for the many gifts bestowed upon them by Grandfather/*Gitche Manitou*/Creator/God through Mother Earth. Socially, pow wows are often the public forum at which ceremonies associated with rites of passage are performed: deaths are announced and the deceased remembered; names are given to individuals; birthdays are celebrated; eagle feathers are passed. Pow wows serve as a means for Indian people to meet new people, to renew old friendships, and to share news and information. Culturally, pow wows provide a means to pass on traditional language, song, dance, crafts, and other customs. Economically, pow wows provide an opportunity for Native Americans to sell food and crafts and to monetarily reward their traditional dancers, singers, and artisans. In short, a pow wow is a time and place to honor past and present community members, to celebrate life and creation, to give thanks, to enjoy the company of family and friends, and to pass on the knowledge of elders to youth.

From Gatherings to Pow Wows: A Brief History of Pow Wows in Michigan

As observed by Vanessa Brown, pow wow dancer, and Barre Toelken, folklorist, "although the inter-tribal pow wow has developed rapidly since the turn of the century as a common form of Native American social expression, surprisingly little has been written about it."[1] The groundbreaking work done in Michigan by Gertrude Kurath and Frances Densmore provides a foundation for the following historical overview of pow wows in this state.[2] Their work is now augmented by the oral histories of the dancers and elders who were interviewed for this project.

Pow wows in Michigan find their historical roots in a variety of traditional gatherings. Here, the People of the Three Fires (Odawa/Ottawa, Potawatomi, and Ojibway/Chippewa), gathered for feasts associated with wild rice and berry harvests, social dances connected with marriages or major rituals, naming ceremonies, funerals and

Joe Chingwa, Harbor Springs, Michigan, n.d. Photo courtesy of Frank Ettawageshik.

Top: Unidentified dancer, probably at Annual Picnic and Pow Wow, Cross Village, Michigan, 1938. Photo courtesy of Frank Ettawageshik.

Bottom: Princess Kishigo, 1948, Harbor Springs, Michigan. Photo courtesy of Frank Ettawageshik.

memorials for the deceased, and meetings of the Wabano and Midewiwin Societies.

During the nineteenth and early twentieth centuries, however, many Great Lakes traditional ceremonies vanished—in whole or in part—for a variety of reasons. Native peoples were forcibly displaced and relocated from their original lands. Children were required to attend mission or government schools (often miles away from their families), where they were forbidden to speak their native language or practice native customs. Native communities were the focus of intense missionary activity by members of Christian denominations. Individuals recruited to these new religions adopted new belief systems, rituals, and ceremonies. Sometimes native beliefs and practices were maintained in tandem with the new religious practices; sometimes observances of Christian holidays were held to coincide with native seasonal activities.

Despite these obstacles to cultural continuity and community cohesion, knowledge of Native American language and individual stories, foodways, songs, dances, and other practices have been maintained. Highly respected elders share their skills and knowledge with new generations, thus ensuring that these traditions will endure. Folklorists, oral historians, and anthropologists record songs, stories, and dances and deposit this information in tribal centers and museums so that future generations will have access to this important legacy. The work of three women—Jane Ettawageshik, Frances Densmore, and Gertrude Kurath—is especially notable for its extensive documentation of songs, dances, and dance regalia.

Regionally and tribally specific dances and songs became less frequently performed as the twentieth century progressed. By the 1950s, when Kurath recorded the Corn Grinding Dance, the Bear Dance, and the White Pigeon, Raccoon, and Hoot Owl songs in Michigan, they were rarely performed. Kurath observed that by the mid-twentieth century, new dances and songs—sometimes borrowed or derived from other tribes in the Great Lakes region and other parts of North America—began to appear more frequently. Thurman Bear, a former Fancy Dancer and a noted pow wow Emcee, remembers traveling with his parents to many gatherings and seeing local dances that are no longer performed. While initially a wide range of different dances were showcased at these gatherings, inter-tribal dances gradually became the most common.

The format of most contemporary pow wows in Michigan is derived from gatherings that have been held by Indians since at least the beginning of this century. Among the first pow wows in

Michigan were those held by the Catholic Ottawa at old Waganakisi—the area of Harbor Springs, Petoskey, and Cross Village. Pageants or shows, organized at first by David Kenosha and later by Susan Shagonaby, were sponsored annually by Catholic Holy Cross Church in Cross Village. By 1960, dancers from local bands and Ottawa communities in southern Michigan had joined with Winnebago dancers from Wisconsin Dells to present a program called "The History of Cross Village" to 3,000 visitors.

In Harbor Springs, a Hiawatha pageant was held as early as 1912 for visitors to the area; this was organized for many years by the Michigan Indian Defense Association. Another pageant, begun in 1954 by a group of Ottawa and directed by Susan Shagonaby, used scripts prepared by Jane Ettawageshik and a large repertoire of choreographed dances by David Kenosha. The cast included members of most of the prominent Indian families in Harbor Springs and Petoskey. Though the pageants are no longer held, Harbor Springs is now home to the Odawa Homecoming, a pow wow that brings together not only members of the local community but also many Odawa who no longer live in Waganakisi.

Another important precedent to the modern format of Michigan pow wows were the programs initiated by a handful of individuals living on the Isabella Reservation near Mt. Pleasant. Led primarily by Eli *(Washsuhkom* or Little Elk) Thomas, these individuals assembled a group of dancers with various tribal and religious affiliations for programs on the reservation and for an annual mid-August program on an old Potawatomi meeting place at Charlton Park near Hastings. As Kurath notes, these inter-tribal gatherings were the occasion for many activities: "In addition to the afternoon and evening performances, there are gatherings for social Indian dances, for story-telling around a fire, and artistic craft displays. . . . The women make and sell Indian corn soup and 'qua bread' [a form of fry bread]."[3] Gifted choreographers and dancers like Benedict Quigno (Potawatomi), Don Otto (Ottawa), James Shaffer (Yamasi Cherokee), and Frank Bush (Potawatomi) joined Thomas in reconstructing old regional dances, introducing dances from other tribal traditions, and developing new dances.

Other gatherings and organizations have played key roles in the evolution of the pow wow in Michigan. Among these are the Indian Village program in Tawas, with dances under the direction of James Shaffer and Allen Rhodes; the Grand Valley American Indian Lodge, with noted singer/dancer John Bosin; and the Grand River American Indian Society. This last group was organized in 1964 by several Indians, including James Shaffer; Jack Neyome; and Betty, Joan, and Judy Pamp, who had danced with Eli Thomas and Anthony Chingman. Many members belong to the Grand River Band of Ottawa; other members must be at least one-quarter Indian. Its first annual pow wow was held in Lansing in 1965.

While most of the early gatherings occurred in rural settings, Detroit boasts one of the oldest and most important urban gatherings. Since 1940, the North American Indian Club has "provided a meeting place for North American Indians to keep alive Indian culture, to promote public understanding of the North American Indian, and to assist Indians to attain higher education."[4] The club's performances of song and dance started out as intimate gatherings for thanksgiving and other special occasions. Its membership now includes Indians from many tribes.

By the early 1970s, pow wows had become quite popular among members of Michigan's native communities. Many current participants recall the growing pains of these years as the pow wow acquired its modern form. Esther (Pekit) Koon remembers with some amusement the first pow wow held in Peshawbestown in 1972. A "Dr. Schroeder," a practicing physician from Northport, urged local Chippewa and Ottawa to have a gathering to remember the traditional dances and songs. Because there was not enough Anishinaabe regalia in the community to outfit all of the interested dancers, he ordered regalia from a catalog on Indian lore. Today, dancers at this now-annual pow wow wear locally made regalia that reflects their own tribal heritage.

Many contemporary Michigan pow wows are held annually; others are held for special occasions. Examples include the Little Elk (Eli Thomas) Retreat held in Mt. Pleasant the first weekend of August; the Leonard J. Pamp Traditional Pow Wow held in Burlington the second weekend of August; the Day of the Eagle Pow Wow held in East Jordan in early June; the Annual Homecoming of the Three Fires Pow Wow held in mid-June in Grand Rapids; the Odawa Homecoming held in Harbor Springs in early August; the Sault Ste. Marie Tribe of Chippewa's Traditional Pow Wow held during the Fourth of July weekend; the Michigan State University NAISO (North American Indian Student Organization) Pow Wow held in East Lansing in February or March; the Michigan State University American Indian Heritage Pow Wow held in East Lansing during the annual Michigan Festival; and the University of Michigan Pow Wow held in Ann Arbor in late March. A complete listing of the state's pow wows is maintained by the Michigan Commission on Indian Affairs.

Contemporary Pow Wows in Michigan

Despite differences in size, venue, and organizing group, most contemporary pow wows in Michigan share certain characteristics. The design of the pow wow site; the composition and responsibilities of the host committee; the sequence of activities; the formalities or rituals enacted; the role of key personnel; the types of songs, dances, and regalia incorporated; and the symbolic nature of the gathering are, with little variation, the same from pow wow to pow wow.

Pow Wow Site Design

Pow wows are often held in the same location year after year. The site must have ground or floor surfaces that are smooth and flat; be large enough to accommodate the dance circle, traders, and audience; and have nearby camping or inexpensive lodging for participants and guests. Ideally, the site features seating in the shade for the audience.

The design and layout of contemporary pow wows reflects symbolism of the pan-Indian, American Indian way of life. The site, whether indoors or outdoors, is based on the circle, which represents unity among American Indians, unity with Mother Earth, the circle of life, the four directions, and the four races of man. The drum, "the heartbeat of the people," is located in the center of the dance arena, preferably under an arbor of cedar boughs. Pow wow emcees, judges, traders, food concessions, and spectators are all arranged in an outer ring surrounding the dance arena.

The Four Directions may be marked in the arena with banners or poles in colors that represent both the cycle of life (birth to death) and the races of man (north/white, south/red, east/yellow, and west/black). The dance arena always opens to the east, the direction in which Indian people look to recognize the beginning of all life.

Pow Wow Roles and Responsibilities

Pow wows in the Great Lakes region are typically organized and governed by a Pow Wow (or Host) Committee. The size of each committee varies according to the needs of the particular Native American community and the size and complexity of the pow wow. Committee members work throughout the year to ensure that their events are successful and that their communities will be proud to sponsor them.

The primary responsibilities of the Host Committee are to choose the date and site of the event and to secure adequate funding for it. If the pow wow is not held on an annual date or weekend, committee members try to select dates that do not conflict with other native events. Depending on size and type, a pow wow can cost as little as $1,000 or many times that; an average pow wow in Michigan costs between $15,000 and $30,000.

The Host Committee selects and prepares a site, lays out the orientation of the arena, builds the cedar arbor, and cleans the site after the gathering is over. Historically, pow wow committees have been responsible for providing campsites and firewood for their guests. This responsibility has diminished in importance as pow wows are more frequently held in urban areas and camping is often prohibited by local government ordinances.

The Host Committee also selects the key personnel for the pow wow, including Emcee, Arena Director, and Head Veteran. If the gathering includes competitive dancing and drum contests, the committee arranges for judges, prizes, and drum and dancer registration. The Emcee (or Master of Ceremonies), handles all announcements during the pow wow and communicates cultural information to the general public. The Arena Director manages the flow of participants into and out of the dance circle throughout the weekend. If the pow wow is competitive, the Arena Director consults with the Head Judge(s) on the sequence of events. The Arena Director also serves as the primary security supervisor for the pow wow. If he deems an individual's conduct unbecoming, he will not allow that person into the arena and may even escort the offender from the pow wow site altogether.

The Head Veteran leads the Grand Entry and is responsible for the care of the eagle feather staff, which is viewed by many as the national flag of Indian nations. The Head Veteran oversees the stewardship of the eagle components of dancers' regalia, and, along with other veterans and the Arena Director, supervises the conduct of pow wow participants.

Competitive pow wows require a Head Judge or Judges, one for men's dances and one for women's dances. Head Judges are selected for their significant pow wow experience and their integrity. They serve as respected role models, devise a scoring system for participating dancers and singers, recruit additional assistant judges, and work closely with the Arena Director and Emcee on the flow of activities.

The Host Committee is responsible for selecting a Host Drum or Drums, who are invited because of their good voices and strong beats. The drum is the symbolic center of events at the pow wow and refers both to the instrument and the group of singers around it. Each drum has a head singer who leads the tribal and pan-Indian songs. Most songs are composed of "vocables," best described as musical sounds emitted from the mouth and emanating from deep within the abdomen. Sixteen common vocables make up the majority of inter-tribal songs. Singers imitate birds or animals and vocalize ancient songs of war and bravery, thanksgiving, and love. The use of vocables helps underscore the feeling of unity among pow wow participants, who may be from tribes that speak different languages.

In addition to singing the Grand Entry Song, the Host Drum sings more frequently than any other drum in attendance. The drum sets the beat for the dancers' rhythms and for changes of dance genres. Drum contests are a regular feature of regional pow wows; sometimes as many as 25 drums compete for cash prizes.

The Host Committee also selects the pow wow's Head Male Dancer and Head Female Dancer. Chosen for their experience and artistry, these dancers lead the other dancers in the Grand Entry procession and, if the pow wow is competitive, in the men's and women's dance contests.

The Host Committee is responsible for providing a "giveaway" at the end of the pow wow that is both a symbolic and a tangible way to honor those who have participated. In Native American cultures, one gains status by sharing or giving away possessions. If feasible, committee members give something to everyone in attendance; gifts are generally useful articles such as clothing, food items, household goods, or tools. Honored guests or dignitaries are presented with gifts of tobacco, blankets, or traditional native craft items such as quilts, sweetgrass or black ash baskets, quillwork, and beadwork.

Pow wows provide an opportunity for American Indians to trade and sell crafts or food items. The Host Committee sets quality standards for the items to be offered and makes all arrangements with vendors. Some family members may participate in dance or drum contests while others tend a sales booth. Few of the craft items offered represent traditions dating to the period before European contact, but most represent skills and design motifs associated with specific tribal groups. Commonly seen in the booths of Michigan pow wow traders are porcupine quill and birchbark containers made by Odawa/Ottawa and black ash splint baskets made by Potawatomi and Ojibwa/Chippewa. In addition to handmade items, traders also offer a wide selection of books, cassette tapes of American Indian music, and miscellaneous items such as t-shirts, lapel buttons, hats, and bumper stickers that proclaim pride in being American Indian.

Perhaps the most common food available at traders' booths is "fry bread"—bread dough deep-fried in fat, served warm, and eaten plain or with a topping such as sugar, jam, or honey. Some Michigan pow wows host fry bread contests and award prizes to the best cooks. "Indian tacos," a variation of Mexican tacos, use fry bread as a base. Another common food is corn soup, traditionally made with hominy, beans, onions, carrots, and beef or pork.

Members of the Host Committee usually provide a hearty meal to all participants on the Saturday evening of a weekend pow wow. This dinner is a way for the committee to show its appreciation for participants who may have had to travel great distances to attend the event. In some areas of the Great Lakes, the meal may include fresh or smoked fish, venison, and other wild game. The committee also provides light snacks, fresh fruit, and beverages for dance participants. Tobacco and asyhma are traditionally given to the drums.

Pow Wow Components and Sequences of Activities

Pow wows in the Great Lakes region are either non-competitive (traditional) or competitive (prizes are awarded to dancers and drums). Generally, they last for two weekend days to accommodate the modern work week. Each pow wow contains slightly different components and sequences of activities that depend on whether the event is competitive and on other factors specific to a particular gathering.

In Michigan, all pow wows are opened formally with a Grand Entry Dance, a single-file processional into and around the dance circle in which all participants are expected to take part. At nearly all pow wows, this processional is led by the Head Veteran, who carries an eagle staff and is accompanied by other veterans who carry the American flag, the Canadian flag, and other flags or staffs deemed appropriate. There is a specific order for the sequence of entry for the remaining participants, but the order varies from tribe to tribe and from one pow wow to the next. In Michigan, it is most common for the veterans to be followed by the Head Male and Head Female Dancers, who are then followed by the male dancers according to age and dance category, always beginning with the Men's Traditional Dancers. Then the women dancers enter the arena, also by age and dance category.

The Grand Entry symbolizes the coming together of American Indians as one people, in unity with Mother Earth and with each other. For participants, it is a time of neutrality when all arguments and harsh feelings toward others are put aside. Because all of the dancers appear in full regalia for the Grand Entry, it is one of the most visually spectacular moments of the pow wow.

When all participants have entered the arena and turned inward toward its center, a Flag Song is sung by the Host Drum. This song is often a tribal anthem or another song that honors the spirit and determination of all people to survive. The AIM (American Indian Movement) Victory Song is sometimes used as a Flag Song; many American Indians consider this song to be their national anthem.

An invocation is then given by a respected elder, usually in the elder's tribal language. The invocation generally includes giving thanks to Grandfather (the creator or God who is considered a member of the family) for the many gifts bestowed upon the Indian people, a blessing on those in attendance and those who are unfortunate, and, if the elder sees fit, commentary on issues of social responsibility or respect. Upon completion of the invocation, the eagle staff and other flags are attached to the side of the cedar arbor. All participants except the drums are then excused from the arena.

After the opening ceremony, many pow wows feature a Veterans' Dance in which only military veterans may participate. Not only does the dance honor these veterans, it also reminds spectators that many Native Americans served in the U. S. armed forces despite the mistreatment they suffered at the hands of the federal government. Another dance that often follows the opening ceremony is the Welcome Dance, which honors those who have traveled far to participate in the pow wow. The Welcome Dance is also a formal welcome to those participants who have not yet been individually greeted by the Host Committee.

These initial dances and songs are followed by a series of inter-tribal songs by each drum in attendance. Then, depending on whether the pow wow is traditional (non-competitive) or competitive, the first round of inter-tribal songs is followed by social, exhibition, or competitive dances interspersed between more inter-tribal songs. Common to all pow wow dances in the Great Lakes region are a consistent drum beat and similar patterns of footwork.

The most common social dances are the Round Dance, Snake Dance, Crow Hops, and Two-step. The Two-step, a ladies' choice, is probably the most frequently performed social dance. "Midnight two-steps" are favorite dances performed late in the evening.

Exhibition dances typically feature the six styles of dance common to Great Lakes competition pow wows: "Traditional" (for men and women), "Fancy" and "Grass" (for men only), and "Fancy Shawl" and "Jingle Dress" (for women only). Occasionally, dances that allow greater latitude in individual expression are seen, including the Hoop, Eagle, and Partridge dances.

Competitive dance categories are broken into age-level groups: Seniors, Adults, Young Adults, Children, and Tiny Tots. Dancers are judged on their overall presentation, their ability to keep time and stop with the drum, and their regalia. Dancers receive cash prizes or payments that represent a kind of reciprocity: it is a way for the Host Committee to acknowledge that the pow wow would not be possible without their participation. At non-competitive pow wows, dancers are generally offered gas money and gifts for their participation.

Special dances known as Honor Dances are commonly held throughout the pow wow weekend in conjunction with announcements or ceremonies honoring one or more individuals. During the Honor Dance, the honorees (and sometimes their families) complete the first circle around the arena. Then all participants may join the dance to help celebrate the occasion or announcement. Following the dances, some pow wows hold a "49" session, during which singing and storytelling take place well into the night. At many pow wows, a giveaway ceremony is held near the conclusion of the two-day event.

During the course of a pow wow, a dancer may inadvertently drop an item or lose a piece of regalia. When this happens, the item is usually picked up by another dancer and given to the Emcee, who announces that the item has been found. The dancer who lost the item redeems it and either voluntarily withdraws or is asked to withdraw from competition. If the item dropped is an eagle feather, a series of ritual activities is immediately undertaken. Until the end of the song, the Head Veteran dances near the feather, protecting it from the stream of dancers moving around it.

At the end of the song, the arena is cleared of dancers and the drum begins an honor song. The Head Veteran and three other veterans approach the feather from the four directions; one of them dances to it and picks it up. For this service the veterans are compensated with a gift from the feather's owner, sometimes with a piece of his regalia. The feather is returned to the owner, or, if he refuses it, is taken care of or given to another dancer by the Head Veteran.

Most regalia (the apparel worn by dancers) is handmade by the dancer or a relative; occasionally, it is obtained through purchase or trade at pow wows. Dance regalia includes headdresses, bustles, jewelry, sashes, dresses, shirts, leggings, shawls, and a variety of handheld items. The clothing usually includes pieces made of materials from the Winged Ones (birds), the Two-Leggeds (man), and the Four-Leggeds (animals). By wearing clothing that contains elements of these natural materials, dancers honor all that gives life on Earth. Dancers and singers in Great Lakes pow wows also make extensive use of the colors red, black, white, and yellow in their regalia and facial adornment. The selection of regalia and the choice of facial adornment are highly personal decisions, and regalia varies greatly from one dancer to the next within parameters that are described in the following pages.

Pow wows are complex and symbolic gatherings for Native Americans in the Great Lakes region. Through participation in pow wows, American Indians nurture their sense of community and publicly affirm their existence as a people while sharing their culture with others.

Notes

[1] Originally an Algonquian term for a curing ceremony, the word "pow wow" has been used historically in different ways. In other parts of North America, contemporary inter-tribal gatherings are sometimes referred to by a local, native term. In Michigan, the word "pow wow" is the most frequently used term for both tribal and inter-tribal gatherings.

[2] See Gertrude Kurath, *Michigan Indian Festivals* (Ann Arbor, Michigan: Ann Arbor Publishers, 1966) and Frances Densmore, *Chippewa Customs* (Minneapolis, Minnesota: Minnesota Historical Society, 1979).

[3] Kurath, 55.

[4] Kurath, 60.

Annual Picnic and Pow Wow to benefit Holy Cross Indian Mission,
Cross Village, Michigan, 1938. Photo courtesy of Frank Ettawageshik.

Dance and Dance Regalia in Michigan

Cameron Wood with Thurman Bear, Jason George, Catherine Gibson, and Bedahbin Webkamigad

Hastings Pow Wow, 1968. Photo courtesy of Charlton Park and Historical Village Museum.

If you can get together one person to sing, one person to dance, one person to pray, one person to carry the flag, and one person to emcee, you've got enough for a pow wow.
Thurman Bear

Pow wows are one of the most vibrant public expressions of a healthy, thriving Native American community. Part ceremony, part family reunion, part public performance, and part county fair, the pow wow is an occasion for a variety of activities. It is an opportunity for native peoples to honor others, to acknowledge their blessings, to share stories, to enjoy each other's company, and to pass on cultural knowledge to younger members of the community. Artists sell their work and vendors serve up "pow wow food," including fry bread and "Indian tacos." Singing and dancing, however, are the heart of the pow wow. Through dance, native peoples express and celebrate their specific tribal and pan-Indian cultures.

Neither of my folks were "pow wow people," but at the time—this was in the early '50s—not many people did pow wows. A lot of people were what I like to call "turning away from the blanket" and there was a lot of pressure then not to do that [go to pow wows].
Thurman Bear

Throughout Native American history, traditional gatherings have been an important part of native culture; music and dance have been critical components of many of these gatherings. Despite attempts by governments and missionaries to suppress Indian gatherings as expressions of "pagan religion," they continued and even flourished within native communities across North America.

Over the years, a new kind of gathering—the pow wow in its modern form—has emerged within native communities. Often pan-Indian in character, these gatherings or pow wows can be found in both urban and rural settings. Over the last 30 years, pow wows have become common among native peoples in Michigan. Nearly every weekend throughout the year, at least one pow wow is taking place somewhere in the state.

Well, a lot of people come to pow wows and they really don't understand what we're doing. I think sometimes the inappropriate behaviors that some people engage in around pow wows—non-Natives— is a factor of their own ignorance. I think that's one of the things that is the primary function of pow wow. When we dance out in the open forum it is to educate the non-Indian people about what our culture is about and to educate them about the beauty of our people and the viability of our culture. And how, if you come looking for Indians acting like Indians in 1868, you're probably not going to find it. You're going to find Indians acting like we act [today], and that's a hard educational bite for some people.

THURMAN BEAR

When I emcee a pow wow I try to pick out somebody in my mind who looks like this is the first time they've been at a pow wow. And I try to introduce what we are doing to this person who has never been there to create an understanding, to dissolve stereotypes, to facilitate the reaching out to each other so when they go home and talk to their friends, their family, their relatives, they will say, "You know, I was at a pow wow last weekend and those Indian people are really friendly. They're really nice. They're really helpful. They really love their culture. They're a very respectful people."

THURMAN BEAR

While pow wows are important gatherings for native peoples, they are also opportunities for non-Natives to learn more about traditional native culture in general and native foods and expressive arts in particular. Non-natives enjoy participating in social and inter-tribal dances and watching the Grand Entry and other dances. Participants and observers marvel at the beauty of the individual dancers and the creativity of the dancers' regalia.

Yeah, making first place, second place, whatever, getting the prize, getting the money, getting the trophy, yeah that counts. That counts. But to step into the arena and to hear that drum start and to know there is just you and a couple of other people in your category, and sometimes when that drum starts, that song reaches inside of me. Like it just reaches in and grabs you. It takes hold of you and it takes you within that song. And you turn yourself loose, you surrender to it. I've seen that happen to other dancers. As an Emcee, to watch a song take over a dancer and when that song is over, when the singers are done and that last drum beat comes and that dancer stops, you know that dancer has had some kind of an experience that only another dancer could understand. That is the beauty of dance. And I'm fortunate that I've had that experience a lot of times where that song gets you.

THURMAN BEAR

In Michigan, as elsewhere, there are two popular types of pow wows: the traditional (or non-competitive) and the competitive. Each type includes dancers and a drum. (The drum refers both to the drum itself and the group of drummers and singers surrounding the drum.) At competitive pow wows, dancers and sometimes drums vie for cash prizes in categories determined by the Pow Wow Host Committee and judged by respected elders. Dancers are judged on their ability to keep time and stop with the drum beat; their creativity, expressiveness, and skill; and their overall presentation, including their dance regalia.

To many people their outfits are a part of them. Some people dreamed of their outfits and they hold special meaning. A lot of people I know, their outfits have been handed down to them from their grandfather or grandmother. These aren't just something we throw together.

BEDAHBIN WEBKAMIGAD

The drum is considered the heartbeat of the pow wow. Dance movements provide a means of expressing stories, feelings, and ideas. A dancer must be careful not to lose the time of the drum, which can often change tempo. If a dancer fails to heed the drum's voice, he or she may miss an important pause. At a traditional pow wow, this means a bit of embarrassment; at a contest pow wow it can mean the difference between winning and losing.

The regalia (or outfits) that dancers wear provide a colorful display for the spectator. Certain dances require specific types of regalia, yet each outfit reflects the creativity of the individual dancer. One set of regalia can include a variety of components: hand-held items, hair styles and ornaments, facial and body decoration, and clothing.

Usually when I sit down and make an outfit I light a smudge or burn tobacco or something. That's where I get my designs from. . . . Well, I realized young that it was a gift, and sometimes people ask me "Will you make me an outfit? I'll pay for it." And I still have a hard time accepting money for something like that. . .because I think it's a gift and I don't want to abuse it. And I think that is the important part. . .you put the love and the prayers and the time into making these outfits, rather than mass-producing them.

CATHERINE GIBSON

The colorful, complex apparel of dancers reflects a variety of traditional artistic skills and knowledge. Sometimes dancers make all of their own regalia; more often, sets of regalia include articles made by a variety of individuals that have been acquired through gift, purchase, or trade.

In almost every case, the regalia is handmade by someone who has learned his or her skills from relatives, friends, and the trial and error of experience. Many regalia pieces include natural materials such as fur, hide, porcupine quills, and feathers; their use demands intricate knowledge of gathering and preparation techniques. Many traditional techniques are used with both natural and commercial materials to fashion regalia items.

When it came time to make an outfit I didn't have anybody to say "This is how it is done." So I'd look at the stuff and go home and mess with it until it came out. I taught myself how to make bustles. I also do some beadwork. I've made aprons, I've made vests, I've made leggings.

THURMAN BEAR

You don't really know all that much about making outfits; but as you get out there and start talking to people, if you ask them the right way—nicely—offer them some tobacco, they'll tell you how to do whatever it is you want to make.

JASON GEORGE

During their long life, regalia items are frequently altered, recycled into new outfits, passed along to another dancer, or traded. Dancers and dance regalia makers often say that their most prized regalia items are not those they have made or purchased, but those they have obtained through trading or bartering with another artist. Trading is considered a practical means of completing an outfit and a way to build good relationships.

On my Fancy Dance outfit I've made and remade every article in my outfit except my roach. I've tried to sit down and tie some porky [porcupine] hair [for the roach] and it just falls apart. My hat's off to someone who can make a roach, I'll tell you that!

THURMAN BEAR

Trading is really fun. I traded [with another artist]. She wanted a set of feathers for her son, and knowing what a good beadworker she was, I cut a deal so that she would make a Fancy Dance beadwork set for my daughter. And so the day we exchanged that stuff I watched her son go dancing away looking over his shoulder just really admiring his feathers—and he was just really into it. And I watched my daughter walk away, looking at her beaded moccasins. Both children were real, real happy with that trade. Everybody won. Never mind that her beadwork far outweighs my featherwork in terms of monetary value. Everybody was happy. So at those points, trading can be really, really fun.

THURMAN BEAR

Sometimes repairs are necessary, especially on moccasins, which take the brunt of the wear and tear of dancing. When a piece of regalia falls off during a competitive dance contest, the dancer may be disqualified; when an eagle feather falls or is dropped, a special ceremony is performed to recover the feather. Thus the regalia maker must take great care in creating outfits that can withstand the vigorous actions of the dancer.

Sometimes I do work on leather, but this particular piece was done on canvas to make it lighter because of all the beads. . . . With this particular outfit, the sole part of the moccasins I replaced three times. And the beadwork, if any of it falls off, then I repair it. Usually when I make an outfit for someone, that's what I tell them. If anything ever falls apart on you, just let me know and I'll repair it for you.

CATHERINE GIBSON

Depending on the type of materials used, the number of components of the regalia, and the amount of decoration used on the components, dance regalia varies greatly in overall weight. A heavy set of regalia makes it difficult to move freely and sustain energetic steps over a long period of time, particularly in hot weather. Sometimes dancers have lighter and heavier sets of regalia and will change sets during the course of a pow wow.

Well, I don't put a label on why I dance. I dance because I enjoy it. It's a part of me and a part of my life. It helps to keep the community together. . .to always remember where we came from and where we are going.

CATHERINE GIBSON

I have my regular family, you know, my immediate family: my mom, my cousins. And then I have my extended family and I have my pow wow family. I could go around and dance and not be worried about anything because I always had auntie and uncles watching out for me. That good feeling I had all through childhood, it strengthened me as a person.

BEDAHBIN WEBKAMIGAD

Dancers and dance regalia makers who participate in pow wows in Michigan affirm their ties both to their own unique tribal heritage and to their identity as part of North America's first peoples. Michigan is home of the Anishnaabeg (the "original men"), as the Ojibwa, Odawa, and Potawatomi collectively refer to themselves. The Anishnaabeg join with members of many other tribes and nations as they participate in the pow wow trail. During pow wow gatherings, they celebrate and express their distinctiveness as individuals, as members of their particular tribal groups, and as members of the greater pan-Indian community.

MEN'S TRADITIONAL DANCE AND REGALIA

CAMERON WOOD WITH STANLEY PELTIER

I do dancing and this was done by the warriors of our people, the men. This is what the regalia represents. They upheld the beliefs that we had. It is made of the animal skins we used to wear, and it also represents preserving our culture and protecting our families and our way of life and so on. Eagle feathers are presented only to those who have done useful things for the people. . . . Veterans are given eagle feathers for some of the deeds they do.

STANLEY PELTIER

The Men's Traditional Dance recounts the action of a warrior or hunter. The dance step is a simple "heel-toe" movement. Dancers keep their bodies in a semi-crouched position, their eyes and head moving quickly as if alert to sounds of enemies or prey. Unlike the Fancy Dancer, the Men's Traditional Dancer keeps his steps near the earth and his body motions somewhat reserved.

As with Women's Traditional Dance regalia, Men's Traditional Dance outfits use only natural materials or those historically associated with European trade. Many traditional dancers incorporate family or clan colors and symbols. Because the dancer represents a warrior, the regalia may also reflect dreams or personal experiences. Although the modern forms of Traditional Dance seen in the Great Lakes region are strongly influenced by the dances of Plains native peoples, the regalia of Anishnaabe traditional dancers reflects their unique heritage.

The regalia that the traditional dancers wear has a lot to do with our beliefs. The colors that we wear with our regalia—with our buckskin—the colors that you see, the beadwork that you see, represents the colors that are ours, just like our Indian names, they are given to us

Above: Traditional Dancer wearing hair roach headdress with two eagle feathers. Annual Homecoming of the Three Fires Pow Wow, Grand Rapids, 1996.

Right: Men's Traditional Dancer Donnie Dowd. Michigan State University American Indian Heritage Pow Wow, East Lansing, 1995.

by the Creator. . . . These colors have meaning. Green represents Mother Earth. These colors [of my regalia] I have because I am Deer Clan. . . they are orange and yellow and white. . . . Those are the colors that are like identification for me. They represent the name.

STANLEY PELTIER

The most common form of head adornment worn by Men's Traditional Dancers is a roach headdress, although animal pelts—especially wolf, coyote, and fox—are also used. Those who can claim distinguished ancestry or membership in certain traditional societies sometimes wear an otter skin turban. Buckskin shirts, yokes, and leggings are important basic features of this regalia. To reflect a connection with the trade goods historically available in the region, dancers in the Great Lakes area often substitute calico or gingham for buckskin shirts and black velveteen for their leggings. Cloth shirts are often decorated with ribbon appliqué across the chest and back. As leggings cover the leg only up to mid-thigh, dancers add an apron or loincloth, now usually worn with Spandex shorts underneath.

Most Traditional Dancers wear a single bustle, attached to a leather belt at the waist and sometimes supported by a suspender-like harness. The bustles are made of dyed goose feathers, hawk feathers, or—for those who have gained sufficient merit—eagle feathers. Footwear (usually moccasins, sometimes Aquasocks or sneakers) complete the basic ensemble.

Men's Traditional Dancer. Detail of Woodlands motif on apron. Annual Homecoming of the Three Fires Pow Wow, Grand Rapids, 1996.

Well, a lot of the outfits that you see have fringes on them. A lot of people think fringes are just decoration but they aren't really, you know. In reality they serve a function as well. A lot of them you see on the shoulder and we wear the shoulder cape and it has fringes as well. If you soak it in the rain, the water doesn't soak into your clothes. It soaks into the fringes and it drips off of the fringes and it keeps you a lot drier.

STANLEY PELTIER

In addition to the basic items listed above, Traditional Dancers from many tribal backgrounds wear or hold a variety of other items to personalize their outfits. These include dance sticks or staffs, clubs, shields, dance fans made from the wing of an eagle or other bird, chokers, earrings, cuffs, and garters. Some dancers also wear face and body paint. Veterans of United States military service often incorporate unit insignia or military decoration into their outfits.

Dance regalia items more closely associated with Eastern Woodlands and Great Lakes tribes include broaches, gorgets, armbands, and other adornments made of silver. Historically, these types of silver pieces were given by both the French and the British to favored Native American leaders and trading partners; sometimes the silverwork was a trophy of battle. Bandolier bags, another popular regional component of traditional dance regalia, have long

*Above: Detail of a bustle. Annual
Homecoming of the Three Fires Pow Wow,
Grand Rapids, 1996.*

*Left: Men's Traditional Dancer. Detail of
roach with bobber and beaded yoke. Sault
Ste. Marie Tribal National Assembly, 14th
Annual Traditional Pow Wow and Spiritual
Conference.*

*Men's Traditional Dancer Nick Chippewa.
Annual Homecoming of the Three Fires Pow
Wow, Grand Rapids, 1996.*

been a feature of Anishnaabe men's clothing. Often the bag is decorated with richly colored floral beadwork designs on a plain white beadwork background. Anishnaabek clothing and personal items often carry a white beaded hem or edging. Plains-style beading characteristically uses geometric designs on a white or light blue background.

I have a medicine bag with me which I wear as a part of my outfit. . .and I carry my tobacco in there and my smudge. . . . Before dancing I smudge my regalia as a purification and also to carry on the tradition. . . . I remember why I wear my outfit. The same with my eagle feathers. I show other people why we carry these eagle feathers. That's what you think about when you smudge your outfit before you go dancing.

STANLEY PELTIER

Top: Men's Traditional Dancer Daniel Pheasant of Manitoulin, Canada. Day of the Eagle Pow Wow, East Jordan, 1996.

Bottom: Men's Traditional Dancer Robert Kewagoshkum of the Grand Traverse Band of Traverse City. Annual Homecoming of the Three Fires Pow Wow, Grand Rapids, 1996.

MEN'S TRADITIONAL DANCE REGALIA

fluffie

roach

neckerchief

choker

vest

bobber

roach spreader

ribbon shirt

breastplate

armband

shield

cuff

bustle

medicine bag

breechcloth

garter

feather fan

leggings

moccasin

WOMEN'S TRADITIONAL DANCE AND REGALIA

CAMERON WOOD WITH BEDAHBIN WEBKAMIGAD AND CATHERINE GIBSON

Above: Women's Traditional Dancer Stella Gibson (right) with her granddaughter Elizabeth Gibson. Michigan State University American Indian Heritage Pow Wow, East Lansing, 1995.

Right: Women's Traditional Dancer Robin Martell. Michigan State University American Indian Heritage Pow Wow, East Lansing, 1996.

I really think it is important that people keep up with their background, their tribal background. So that's why I, when I make beadwork for myself, I tend to stick to Woodlands-style floral designs.

BEDAHBIN WEBKAMIGAD

While the Men's Traditional Dance celebrates man's role as warrior or illustrates a story from the life of a particular individual, the Women's Traditional Dance exemplifies the Anishinaabe ideal of woman as lifegiver, caregiver, teacher, and guardian of Indian culture and heritage.

A good Women's Traditional Dancer seems relaxed yet dignified; the dance steps are very reserved. The dancer usually holds her upper body still, occasionally dipping at the knees and bending at the waist in acknowledgment of the honor beats of the drum. Stepping softly upon the ground, reflecting her reverence for Mother Earth, the dancer moves in place or in a very slow progression around the dance arena.

Women's Traditional Dance regalia usually represents a strong link to the dancer's tribal heritage. Dance regalia made or worn by Anishnaabe or other Woodlands Indian dancers often includes ribbonwork, beadwork, and quillwork in floral designs. The outfit is also a statement of personal expression, and the colors or patterns chosen often have deep personal meaning for the dancer.

Once, when I was little, this woman came up to me—she knew my family—and she said, "I've been watching you dance this weekend and I like how you dance, and I want to give you this gift." And it was a plastic freezer bag, one of those huge ones, full of real bone, the long ones [hairpipe beads] for a breastplate. And I remember I started crying

because I had wanted a breastplate. I saw other people with their real bone breastplates and it just came out of nowhere. Things like that I really appreciate, and so that's how my outfits have come together, through family and giveaways.

BEDAHBIN WEBKAMIGAD

The primary components of a Women's Traditional Dance outfit include a shawl, purse, feather fan, and either a one-piece dress, blouse and skirt, or yoke and skirt. Odawa or Ojibwa dresses usually have a decorative ribbon appliqué at the chest and sometimes at the back. Potawatomi Women's Traditional Dancers prefer a blouse with a large ruffle around the shoulders and a straight skirt with appliquéd hem. The shawl, carried folded over one arm, represents the shielding from harm that a mother provides to her children. In the other hand, the dancer carries the purse and feather fan. Other components include footgear (usually moccasins, occasionally sneakers or Aquasocks), earrings, necklaces, and breastplates that sometimes reach the knees or even the ankles. A dancer's hair is worn loose or in long braids with a single feather and hair ties.

I started so young. . .I do remember starting to realize how much effort it took to put together an outfit. I remember I was probably about seven when I started wanting to help put together my outfits. I learned sewing from my mom and my dad helped me learn how to work with hides and make chokers. All my brothers and I were taught how to sew and all of us can get by doing some beadwork.

BEDAHBIN WEBKAMIGAD

The regalia of Women's Traditional Dancers is generally made of natural materials, including hide, buckskin, megis shells, feathers, and porcupine quills. These are supplemented or occasionally replaced with other materials, such as glass beads, silver, wool, velvet, and calico, historically available through trade with Europeans. More recently available or less expensive items such as plastic beads or sequins are also used.

Women's Traditional Dancer Renee Wemigwans. Annual Homecoming of the Three Fires Pow Wow, Grand Rapids, 1996.

*Women's Traditional Dancers JoAnn
Whitehouse (left) and Bedahbin
Webkamigad (right). Michigan State
University American Indian Heritage
Pow Wow, East Lansing, 1996.*

*Women's Traditional Dancers.
From left to right: Buckskins,
Robin Bush, Elizabeth Gasco,
Stella Gibson. Annual
Homecoming of the Three Fires
Pow Wow, Grand Rapids, 1996.*

*Women's Traditional Dancers. Left
to right: Bedahbin Webkamigad,
Terry Weller, and an unidentified
woman. Michigan State University
American Indian Heritage Pow
Wow, East Lansing, 1996.*

Women's Traditional Dancer Terry Weller (center). Michigan State University American Indian Heritage Pow Wow, East Lansing, 1996.

As with all types of dance regalia, the production of a Women's Traditional Dance outfit demands much skill, knowledge, and dedication. The materials must first be acquired and prepared, then fashioned into the elaborately constructed and decorated outfits. The wide variety of techniques and materials used in the construction of an outfit reflects a level of expertise usually acquired over many years of experience. Beadwork, a popular method of applying color and design, may, by itself, incorporate many different techniques and stitches.

I know there are several styles of how people put their beads on. I commonly do four beads and then go back through and tack down two. So it takes me a little longer but it holds better [and] it looks better. You have to be careful on velvet.

BEDAHBIN WEBKAMIGAD

You have to have a strong thread. You can't use regular thread because some of the beads have sharp edges and they'll cut right through it. . . . [I use] nylon and then use beeswax to coat it so the thread will last longer and it doesn't rot.

CATHERINE GIBSON

WOMEN'S TRADITIONAL DANCE REGALIA

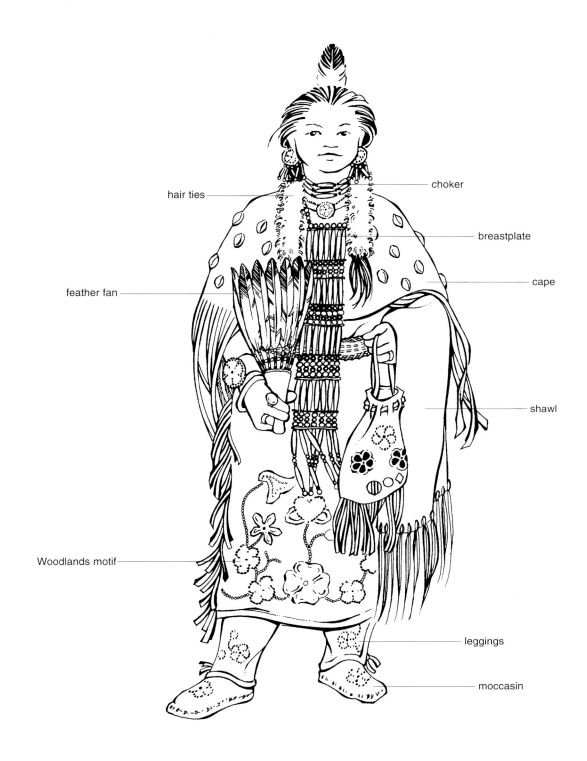

hair ties

choker

breastplate

feather fan

cape

shawl

Woodlands motif

leggings

moccasin

JINGLE DRESS DANCE AND REGALIA

CAMERON WOOD WITH ELIZABETH OSAWAMICK

[The jingle dress] is a healing dress and a very special dress. The healing and teaching behind it. . .[includes this story that] there was a grandchild that was sick and her grandfather didn't know what to do. And one day that grandfather had a dream of that girl; she was to wear a dress covered with bright cones. And in that dream that girl, the grandchild, would be healed. Each cone represents each day of the year, the 365 cones that I mentioned. This dress is seen as a healing dress and it is greatly respected. So this is the story of the jingle dress.

ELIZABETH OSAWAMICK

Although the details of the birth of the jingle dress vary depending on the storyteller, the origin of the dance as described by Osawamick is universal among the Anishinaabeg. The grandfather (in some versions, this figure is a young woman) dreams of the dress in the early 1900s, one of the most difficult periods in the Anishinaabeg's long history. The number of Native Americans and their level of prosperity were at their lowest ebb. Like the Ghost Dance and the Dream Dance, the Jingle Dress Dance shows the fierce determination of Native peoples to deal with hardship.

At the pow wow, Jingle Dress Dancers have two distinct styles of dance. For competition or for inter-tribal dances, the steps include

Left: Jingle Dress Dancer Briana Johnson of the Tuscarora Nation of Ontario. Grand Entry, Morning Star Traditional Pow Wow, Muskegon, 1996.

Right: A Jingle Dress Dancer in an inter-tribal dance. Sault Ste. Marie Tribal National Assembly, 14th Annual Traditional Pow Wow and Spiritual Conference, 1996.

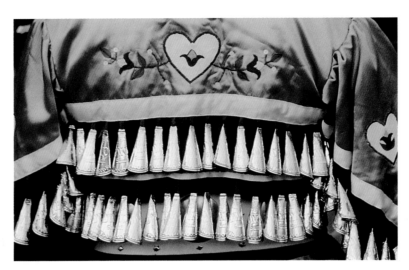

delicate regular and cross steps, sometimes performed in a very intricate pattern. Alternatively, the Jingle Dress Dancers face the center of the arena and slowly circle it with low, short sidesteps. When the Emcee calls for a healing dance or an individual dancer is asked for a healing prayer, the dancer thinks of whom she prays for, sending good thoughts along with the wafting of the fan she carries. The cones make a musical "jingle" sound, attracting the attention of the spirits to answer the dancer's prayers. When a number of Jingle Dress Dancers are in time with the drum, the sound is especially impressive.

I have the jingle dress itself, she ba shegoning ma goodoss, *that's the jingle dress. I have leggings, moccasins, a beaded belt, hair ties, a barrette, an eagle feather—*migisi migwan—*and I usually wear rings on each hand. My first dress was made by Marie Eshkabuck, my cousin, and she made my dress from broadcloth and cones. . . . Then the beadwork that I made for myself, I made my own purse. . .it's a medicine purse and I keep my medicines in there, the four medicines. The first dress that I have, it's red and blue and green and I've used those colors for a reason. Those colors are Midewewin colors. The red represents the blood of Mother Earth, the blue represents water. And the green represents the plant life.*

Elizabeth Osawamick

Jingles were originally made from deer hooves; today metal tobacco can lids are twisted into cones. Although the twisting is sometimes still done by hand, machine-made jingles are now commercially produced and commonly available. The dress can be made from broadcloth or satin, usually with two or three basic colors, sometimes trimmed with appliquéd designs. Buckskin leggings and moccasins, in many cases with intricate beading or sequin work, cover the legs. A wide belt of leather with beadwork or trade silver circles is used to cinch the dress at the waist. Hair ties and barrettes, often with a single feather, complement braided hair. A purse or bag to carry one's medicines and a feather fan complete the ensemble.

Top: Jingle Dress Dancer. Grand Entry, Michigan State University American Indian Heritage Pow Wow, East Lansing, 1996.

Bottom: Jingle Dress Dancer. Grand Entry, Michigan State University American Indian Heritage Pow Wow, East Lansing, 1996.

When a person wants to dance the jingle dress. . .because it's a sacred dress, they have to really think about it. They can't just go out and dance. It has to be given through a dream or they have to be really inspired. If you didn't have that dream you have to fast for that dress. They can't abuse their bodies when they dance. What I mean is that they can't take alcohol or drugs while they're wearing this dress. . .they can't be doing it at all. Whatever outfits we wear, especially the jingle dress, we have to smudge ourselves, smudge our outfits after we have them on. And that's another teaching that was given. . .and we've got to respect that teaching.

ELIZABETH OSAWAMICK

Jingle Dress Dancers with Briana Johnson of the Tuscarora Nation of Ontario in the middle. Grand Entry, Morning Star Traditional Pow Wow, Muskegon, 1996.

WOMEN'S JINGLE DRESS DANCE REGALIA

neckerchief

slide or bolo

hair ties

jingle dress

jingle

leggings

moccasin

Fancy Shawl Dance and Regalia

Cameron Wood with Netawn Alice Kiogima

The Fancy Shawl Dance represents the butterfly, the wings of a butterfly. And when that shawl dancer is dancing, it's like they're rejoicing for a warrior or a loved one that is on his or her way to the spirit world. So it is like we are happy for that person. We're sad—we're mourning—but then we open our wings and we are happy that that person is going to the spirit world. That was the story I was taught about the Fancy Shawl.

Netawn Alice Kiogima

The Fancy Shawl Dance evolved over the last 30 years out of the desire of young Native American women to "kick up their heels" at dances. In the 1960s, women began to use a more energetic step than usual in the Women's Traditional Dance and even sometimes slipped into Men's Fancy Dance competitions. By the mid-1970s, they had created a separate dance—the Fancy Shawl Dance. Dancers wore the shawl around their shoulders and used intricate and active steps. Unlike the Women's Traditional Dance, in which the feet of the

Left: Fancy Shawl Dancer. Sault Ste. Marie Tribal National Assembly, 14th Annual Traditional Pow Wow and Spiritual Conference, 1996.

Right: Fancy Shawl Dancer. Sault Ste. Marie Tribal National Assembly, 14th Annual Traditional Pow Wow and Spiritual Conference, 1996.

dancer do not leave the earth, the Fancy Shawl Dance requires spins, hops, and cross steps. Where the Women's Traditional Dancer avoids movements that reveal her legs, the Women's Fancy Dancer swirls her skirt about, revealing brightly beaded or sequined leggings underneath. Although this sometimes causes a bit of consternation among the older generation, the Fancy Shawl Dance requires a great deal of endurance from the dancer, who has to keep her energy up for many rounds of dancing over a weekend.

I have four [outfits]. On Sundays I try to go from the heaviest outfits to the lightest. I'll start off with my beadwork and then I'll go to my sequins. Because at the end of the pow wow I'm really tuckered out but you usually have contests every session. There are no limitations of what you can do to your outfit. It's whatever your personality is and what your taste is. There is not a set way you have to be; but you do have to have your basics.

Netawn Alice Kiogima

The Fancy Shawl Dance regalia consists of many of the same items found in a Women's Traditional outfit, although in a brighter, more "modernized" form. The shawl is made of cotton or other light fabric and is usually decorated with appliquéd ribbonwork and fringe. Most dresses are made of satin, which is lightweight, flows with the dancer's movements, and has a "shiny" surface finish that attracts the viewer's eye. Both one-piece dresses and skirts with yokes are used. Leggings extend from mid-calf to knee length, depending on the individual's preference. Appliquéd ribbonwork, beadwork, and sequin decorations may be used in any combination. Sequins are very popular for Fancy Shawl Dance regalia because they are lighter in weight than beads and reflect the light, creating a "flashy" look. Hair ties and barrettes are worn in the dancer's braided hair, which is often adorned with a single feather. Because the dancers hold the ends of the shawl with both hands, Fancy Shawl Dancers do not carry any hand-held items.

I decided to become a Fancy Shawl Dancer and we started going to more pow wows and looking at Fancy Shawl Dancers—their outfits. I decided on floral beadwork, more of a Great Lakes design. My mother was drawing out these different flowers. Well, one of those I really liked and I asked her if I could use that for my first outfit. Then I picked out my colors and my aunt drew it out on canvas and then we started beading. Then my grandma got in on it, my mother got in on it, and I got in on it. . .and one of my sisters helped draw another flower. So it was that my first outfit is the most special and most powerful to me because it has got all the power of the women in my family into one outfit.

Netawn Alice Kiogima

Fancy Shawl Dancer Eva Oldman of Harbor Springs. Sault Ste. Marie Tribal National Assembly, 14th Annual Traditional Pow Wow and Spiritual Conference, 1996.

*Above: Fancy Shawl Dancer. Sault Ste. Marie Tribal
National Assembly, 14th Annual Traditional Pow Wow
and Spiritual Conference, 1996.*

*Below: Fancy Shawl Dancer Melanie Matthews of
Albuquerque, New Mexico. 19th Annual Lansing
Indian Contest Pow Wow, 1996.*

Like other types of dance regalia, the Fancy Shawl Dance regalia often incorporates floral patterns in the beadwork or sequin work. The design and construction of an outfit usually involves several members of a dancer's circle of family and friends.

It would be so awkward for me not going to a pow wow or not going to a Native function where there's art and music and meeting other people and family members. I thank the Creator every day for making me an Anishinaabe que [Native American woman]. I couldn't ask to be anything more.

NETAWN ALICE KIOGIMA

Above: Close-up of beaded yoke. Michigan State University American Indian Heritage Pow Wow, East Lansing, 1996.

Below: Lisa Ojibway. Michigan State University American Indian Heritage Pow Wow, East Lansing, 1996.

WOMEN'S FANCY SHAWL DANCE REGALIA

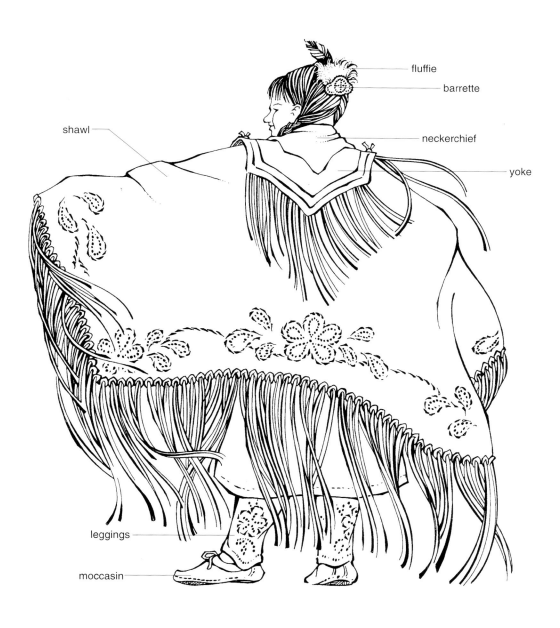

fluffie

barrette

shawl

neckerchief

yoke

leggings

moccasin

GRASS DANCE AND REGALIA

CAMERON WOOD WITH CATHERINE GIBSON

It is generally believed that the Grass Dance originated among Plains native peoples. By the late 1800s, it had spread to the Anishinaabe of the Great Lakes area. Both the steps and the regalia of the Grass Dance reinforce a symbolic association with the prairie. While the dancer sways his upper body back and forth, he takes a short step with one foot and then drags the other foot forward in a long, lazy arc. Dancers often say that this unique step was designed to flatten the prairie grass in the dance circle for the other dances that followed. Other research suggests that the name "Grass Dance" comes from the historical Plains tradition of dancers placing bundles of grass in their belts. Today the grass is represented by long strips of cloth, yarn, leather, or ribbon fringes that trim or sometimes completely cover the outfit. When the dancer moves, the fringes sway, mimicking the flowing grasses of the Great Plains.

Left: Grass Dancer Dallas Soney. Michigan State University American Indian Heritage Pow Wow, East Lansing, 1995.

Right: Grass Dancer Dennis Shananaquet. Michigan State University American Indian Heritage Pow Wow, East Lansing, 1995.

The original fringe was leather and I guess the reason why I switched it to yarn is because that's the norm for grass dancers. I know now they're using ribbon—my son's outfit has ribbons on it. And I met a guy out in North Dakota and he was in his early 70s. He had a grass dance outfit when he was younger and they used to tear old cloth and make it out of rags. He said that was the original dance outfit—[it] was just old material and it was torn to look like fringe. And they called them rag dancers, from what I understand. But now I've seen, so far, three guys that have the material torn.

CATHERINE GIBSON

The yoke or shirt and apron can be of any material, but lighter fabrics are preferred because they keep the dancer cool. The outfit is usually decorated with lightweight appliqué ribbonwork; heavier beaded outfits are also worn. Accessories common to other styles of men's dance—such as a porcupine roach headdress, moccasins, feather fan, chokers, and beaded cuffs—are also used. Most Grass Dancers wear the angora leg coverings, bells, and twirlers also used by Fancy Dancers. Absent are the bustles worn by Traditional and Fancy Dancers, since these would interfere with the waving motion

Boy's Grass Dancer Kyle Crawford. Morning Star Traditional Pow Wow, Muskegon, 1996.

Above: Grass Dancer Nate Gibson
(Odawa). Michigan State University
American Indian Heritage Pow Wow, East
Lansing, 1995.

Right: Grass Dancer Paul Shananaquet.
Michigan State University American
Indian Heritage Pow Wow, East Lansing,
1995.

created by the fringes and the dancer's movement. Almost all Grass Dancers carry either a hoop of braided sweetgrass or wear a braid of sweetgrass attached to the back of their outfit.

Actually that started out to be a Fancy Dance outfit for my brother and he switched styles of dancing from Fancy to Grass and, with the help of his mother-in-law, [the Fancy Dance outfit] was turned into a Grass Dance outfit. But the design and everything was my original design. All the beadwork was used. I don't know what he did with the rest of the stuff, but yeah, all the beadwork was used.

CATHERINE GIBSON

Above: Grass Dancer Nate Gibson (Odawa). Michigan State University American Indian Heritage Pow Wow, East Lansing, 1995.

Left: Grass Dancer Dennis Shananaquet. Michigan State University American Indian Heritage Pow Wow, East Lansing, 1995.

GRASS DANCE REGALIA

roach

bobber

hairpin

rosette

headband

drops

neckerchief

yoke

choker

sash

cuff

dance stick

sweetgrass

apron

hoop

moccasin

49

Fancy Dance
and Regalia

Cameron Wood with
Jason George

*This is how it was told to me. . .It [the Fancy Dance] came out of the
Grass Dance or Helushka tradition. . .I think that's Pawnee or Omaha,
and it was specifically a warrior dance. . . . Men were supposed to
express themselves. . . . The grass dancers from that time—the late
1800s and early 1900s—would go into a wild west show, Buffalo Bill's
Wild West Show. And I guess Buffalo Bill went to them one day and
said "Can't you do something more exciting? I mean, don't get me
wrong, I like your dancing and all; but maybe pick up the tempo or
something like that." Of course, those guys being Indian and all, [they]
could adapt. And they said "Sure, we can do something like that." So
they put a few more moves in and made it faster and they ended up
getting Fancy Dancers.*

Jason George

No other style of American Indian dance has such widespread
popularity among native peoples across the country than the Fancy
Dance. Its regalia has become the pervasive outfit of the Pan-Indian
dancer. While Buffalo Bill's Wild West Show may not have been the
only reason for the creation of the Men's Fancy Dance, it does reflect
the desire of young men to have a showier, more athletic dance and
the desire of an outside audience for a "better show." Today, pow

*Above: Fancy Dancers. Sault Ste. Marie
Pow Wow, 1996.*

*Below: Two Fancy Dancers. Sault Ste.
Marie Tribal National Assembly, 14th
Annual Traditional Pow Wow and
Spiritual Conference, 1996.*

*Right: Men's Fancy Dancer Frank
Buswa. Sault Ste. Marie Pow Wow,
1996.*

Feather bustles in motion. Michigan State University American Indian Heritage Pow Wow, August 1996.

wow emcees will often note this fact for the audience, emphasizing that Native Americans are very much "with it" and interested both in maintaining old traditions and creating new forms of performance and regalia.

Although seldom a distinct category at pow wows until the 1960s, the Fancy Dance began to come into its own in the 1930s when shoulder and wrist bustles began to appear as part of the regalia. Gradually outfits became more extravagant in appearance. Porcupine and deer hair roaches, or "porky roaches," are the most common headdress. The deer hair is often bleached or dyed different colors, with matching or complementary bases of woven yarn. The base is often covered with a roach spreader made of silver, and one or two feathers mounted on bobbers are added to this. The roach is held in place with a hairpin and chin tie of leather. A headband, made using the loom beading technique, is usually worn. This headband often has a quilled or beaded rosette and two loom-beaded drops.

When you make an outfit, you make it over a long period of time. You make a little bit here, and add it to your outfit, make a little bit there, and soon you'll have a complete outfit. It takes a while to get the money, and then it takes a while to get the materials to make it. So it takes a while to get it right.

JASON GEORGE

The most striking feature of the Fancy Dance regalia are the large bustles. These are usually "swing" bustles, made to allow the feathers to swing back and forth with the dancer's movement. In contrast, many Traditional Dance bustles have the feathers firmly affixed to the center of the bustle, which prevents them from moving independently. The bustles are held in place on the dancer by a harness, which is frequently decorated with loom beading, mirrors, or silver work. They are then tucked under a wide belt. Like the harness, the

Above: Fancy Dancers. Sault Ste. Marie Tribal National Assembly, 14th Annual Traditional Pow Wow and Spiritual Conference, 1996.

Below: Fancy Dancer. Michigan State University American Indian Heritage Pow Wow, East Lansing, 1996.

belt is often beaded. Most dancers wear a T-shirt underneath the harness.

Many Fancy Dancers wear a yoke decorated with appliquéd ribbonwork. An apron, often decorated with appliquéd ribbon, is usually worn around the waist, with Spandex tights worn underneath. Angora anklets decorated with large sheep bells add a silvery accompaniment to the drum beat. Beaded moccasins complete the basic regalia. Among the numerous accessories often included in the Fancy Dance regalia are beaded or appliquéd cuffs, chokers or neckerchiefs, breastplates, and earrings. All fancy dancers use twirlers. The whole assemblage usually features one or two favorite colors of the wearer.

Fancy Dancer Frank Buswa. Sault Ste. Marie Tribal National Assembly, 14th Annual Traditional Pow Wow and Spiritual Conference, 1996.

Wands, or twirlers, are like sticks with feathers put on strings. Really they were whips at one time, you know, horse whips, and they carried them with them. It adds more movement when you're dancing. A lot of them are made really different. Some people weigh them down with whatever comes to hand, like say, lug nuts. The most recent pair I saw used dowels—dowels with feathers. Weighed 'em down real good. They were really cool and they spun well, too.

JASON GEORGE

Some parts of the Fancy Dance regalia fall in and out of fashion. Arm bustles, which were popular in the 1930s and 40s, fell out of favor in the 50s and 60s, and are now once again commonly used. Indeed, the one constant seems to be an ever more flamboyant assemblage. Although some dancers use relatively sedate imitation eagle feathers (actually goose feathers) that are white with brown tips, many now prefer more garishly colored feathers. Bright circles of felt are commonly added to the tips, along with fluffies and horse hair or ribbon streamers.

Fancy Dance steps and regalia are flamboyant. Jumps, spins, and rapid movements are the norm as young men try to outdo one another. The quivering back shoulder bustles and arm bustles, the hand-held and decorative twirlers, the waving handkerchiefs, and the use of shiny materials such as sequins and compact discs add to the impression of nonstop motion created by the dancer.

FANCY DANCE REGALIA

roach

turban

bustle

rosette

epaulette

harness

cuff

twirler

anklet

goats

moccasin

Glossary of Regalia Items, Materials, and Techniques

Marclay Crampton and Frances Vincent

The following selective glossary provides brief definitions of individual items, materials, and techniques commonly used in contemporary Great Lakes pow wow regalia.

ITEMS

Beaded apron with Woodlands floral motif

Anklet: Woven or leather accessory, often decorated with bells, worn at the ankle or below the knee.

Apron: A garment common to all men's dance regalia, an apron is made of leather and/or cloth and worn free-hanging, front and back, suspended from the waist. It is decorated with beadwork, appliqué, fringe, and pins. On Fancy and Grass Dancers, the apron and yoke often match. In contest pow wows, the competitor's identification number will usually be pinned here.

Armband: An article that encircles the upper arm biceps. Depending on the regalia style, armbands vary from simple to elaborate and use a wide variety of materials for construction, including metal, leather, textile, fur, feathers, beads, bone, and ribbon. They may be adorned with design motifs and colors to match other regalia items.

Bandolier bag: This pouch with a strap is usually worn by Men's Traditional Dancers at the hip, with the strap extending diagonally across the chest and over the shoulder. Both strap and pouch are commonly decorated with fur, fringe, and motifs in beadwork and quillwork.

Beaded barrette/hairslide with feather

Barrette: An object frequently worn singly or in sets in the hair of women dancers. Barrettes are metal, wood, or bone pieces decorated with beadwork, quills, feathers, fur, bone, or antler.

Bobber: A wire apparatus incorporated into the hair roach or bustle that is used to keep attached feather(s) in an upright position.

Bolo tie: A leather thong or braid held together with a decorated slide and worn around the neck.

Breastplate

Close-up of bustle

Dance staff

Epaulet or epaulette

Breastplate: An object simulating body armor, constructed of bone tubes arranged vertically or horizontally, and worn on the upper chest. On men a breastplate extends from collar to waist; on women it extends to dress hem length.

Breechcloth: See Apron, Trade wool, or Loincloth.

Bustle: A large disc with protruding feathers worn by Male Traditional and Fancy Dancers. It hangs off the back and is suspended from the waist. Fancy dancers wear an additional bustle on the shoulders.

Cape: A textile worn by women around the shoulders and adorned with designs in beadwork, quills, sequins, and fringe.

Crown: A beaded and/or quilled headpiece worn by the dancer designated as "Tribal Princess."

Choker: A band worn around the neck. Men's chokers are made of bone, beads, and leather; women's chokers are made of dentalium, beads, and leather.

Clubs: Gunstock, ball, see Dance staff.

Cuffs: Apparel decorated with beadwork, quillwork, and often fringe that encircles the wrists. Often the design and color of the cuffs match those of the belt, yoke, cape, and apron.

Dance staff or Dance stick: A hand-held article commonly used by Men's Traditional Dancers. Constructed from wood, gunstock, antler, and leather, the dance staff is often decorated with beadwork, quills, feather(s), metal, fringe, fur or hair, bone, and ribbon. Sometimes referred to as a coup stick.

Drops: Loom-beaded tassels attached to a headband and used to support a porcupine roach.

Eagle staff: Commonly called the "Indian Flag," the eagle staff is a large wooden pole, approximately eight feet long, adorned with eagle feathers arranged vertically along its length.

Epaulet(s) or Epaulette(s): A decoration with feathers worn on the shoulder in place of, or in combination with, a man's yoke.

Feather fan: Hand-held fan used by both men and women dancers. Constructed primarily of the wing feathers of a bird of prey (eagle, hawk, or falcon), the feather fan is decorated with motifs in beadwork, quills, fringe, leather, and ribbon. Commonly used with dance staff, club, rattle, and prayer hoop.

Fluffie: A slang term for the puffy natural or artificial breast feathers used to accent bustles or headdresses.

Garter: Leg decoration worn immediately below the knee, encircling the calf. Often worn in sets with leggings, garters are decorated with beadwork, quills, bells, cones, deer toes, fringe, conchos, and ribbon.

Hair ties

Goats: An anklet made of long, shaggy goat hair, worn around the calves as a leg ornament by male dancers.

Gorget: Commonly constructed of crescent-shaped metal and often decorated with incised designs, the gorget is worn at the throat as a piece of simulated armor by both men and women.

Hair comb: Hair adornment worn by women, often with feathers, and decorated with beadwork, quills, ribbon, and sequins.

Hair tie(s): Any of many materials or techniques used to secure the hair of both men and women.

Hair pin: Small wood or bone stick, one to eight inches in length, used by men to secure a roach to the scalp and by women to secure a barrette to the scalp.

Harness: A belt and suspenders arrangement designed to support a dance bustle. The harness is often decorated with beadwork or trade silver.

Hoop: A circle, usually made from sweetgrass or red willow, often divided into quarters. Carried in the hand or attached to regalia, the hoop is a symbolic representation of the harmonious cycle of seasons, the four directions, and other Native American traditional concepts that incorporate four aspects or elements.

Medicine bag

Jingle dress: A one-piece dress or matching blouse and skirt, commonly constructed of cotton calico or satin and adorned with jingles. Sometimes as many as 365 jingles, representing the days of the year, are used on one outfit. The jingle dress is the primary garment of the Jingle Dress Dance regalia.

Leggings: Decorated and fringed garment worn on the legs. Men's leggings extend from the thigh to the ankle. Women's leggings commonly begin just below the knee.

Medicine bag: A pouch usually made of animal hide. Bags of the Midé (Grand Medicine Society) are made of an entire otter skin that is worn tucked under and over the belt. Smaller individual medicine bags are worn around the neck, wrist, shoulder, or on the hip.

Medicine wheel: A wooden hoop, usually made of willow. Sometimes called a prayer hoop, it is often held together with a feather fan, club, pipe, purse, staff, or rattle.

Neckerchief

Moccasin: A word of Algonquian origin, literally meaning shoe. Specifically, it refers to a flexible sole leather shoe worn by Native Americans from many tribes. There are several styles of moccasins. Historically, the style of a particular "moc" was an indication of the tribal affiliation of the wearer. The word "Ojibwa," which translates as "puckered up," refers to the particular type of moccasin that was worn by members of that nation. Typically the uppers of the shoe are soft buckskin and the sole is a heavier, tougher material such as moose hide leather.

Neckerchief: A cloth scarf worn in the fashion of a bolo tie around the neck.

Shawl

Shield

Roach

Sash

Pipe: Also known as a calumet, a pipe is frequently made from catlinite, a red-colored stone. Ceremonial and cultural importance is associated with the pipe.

Pipe bag: A leather or cloth bag used to transport the pipe.

Rattle: A noisemaker constructed of turtle shell, horn, rawhide, wood, or gourd with seeds or beads inside. Hand-held or attached to articles of regalia, the rattle carries ceremonial importance.

Ribbon shirt: A long-sleeved shirt commonly constructed of cotton calico or satin that is adorned with appliquéd ribbons. The ribbon shirt is the primary undergarment of the Men's Traditional Dance regalia.

Roach: A men's hairpiece made of the guard hairs of the porcupine and commonly adorned with one or two eagle feathers. It gives its wearer the look of a Mohawk haircut (the hair shorn close to the scalp except for a central swathe at the crown of the head).

Roach spreader: An implement used to vary the angle of the porcupine hairs on a roach; made of metal, leather, or other stiff yet pliable material.

Rosette: A round, stylized floral design that is beaded, painted, or quilled; found in the center of bustles, headbands, aprons, capes, yokes, and armbands.

Sash: A hand-woven belt made of colorful cord or yarn. It is worn around the waist or over the shoulder, usually by men but occasionally by women.

Shawl: Worn over the shoulders or folded across the arm, the shawl is an essential part of all styles of women's dance regalia. Shawls, constructed out of a variety of fabrics, are often extensively fringed and decorated with appliqued fabric or beadwork. Leather shawls are sometimes used by Traditional Dancers, as are trade blankets.

Shield: Usually seen on the arm of the Men's Traditional Dancer; smaller versions can be seen on women. The shield is usually a flat, leather surface emblazoned with an image of the tribal, clan, or personal totem of the wearer. The shield carries great spiritual importance.

Slide or bolo: An item, usually ornamented, with a hole or loop through which a handkerchief or a braid or strip of leather is pulled to create a necktie.

Turban: A cotton cloth swaddled around the top of the head, the turban is an uncommon men's head covering. It is often adorned with a feather, rosette, and trade silver.

Twirlers or wands: Hand-held sticks decorated with colorful streamers, twirlers are used most often by Men's Fancy Dancers to accentuate their body movements. Less colorful wands can be found in the regalia of Men's Traditional Dancers.

Yoke

Vest: A textile and/or leather garment commonly used in the Men's Traditional Dance regalia. It is often decorated with combinations of beadwork, quills, and appliqué.

Yoke: A textile piece most often seen in Men's Grass Dance regalia, the yoke rests loosely on the shoulders. It sometimes uses the same motifs and colors as the apron, and can be extensively fringed.

MATERIALS

Antler: A type of bone that is grown and then shed annually by members of the deer family. Antlers are used whole as decorations on dance sticks, bustles, or headdresses or sliced into discs for use as buttons or dangles.

Bead: One of the primary materials used to create decorative elements in nearly all dance regalia articles. Commercially available and commonly used glass and plastic beads range in size from 1 mm to 20 mm. Other bead materials are shell, metal, bone, antler, stone, and horn. Different types of beads are also called French, Czech, seed, pony, crow, cut glass, metal shot, wampum, and trade.

Beads worked in a Woodlands floral motif used to decorate a cuff

Bell: Manufactured in a variety of different sizes and metals, the bell is used in all facets of regalia construction. It is often seen on the bands worn around the ankles or calves of the Men's Traditional Dancer.

Bone: A dense, calcified tissue that provides the supporting skeleton of vertebrates. Bone appears in regalia in a variety of forms. It is the primary material used to make hairpipe beads for breastplates. Sometimes the wing bones of eagles are used to make whistles, which are considered sacred instruments.

Catlinite: A stone that can be carved to fashion a calumet or pipe. Its common name is pipestone and it can be found in southwest Minnesota.

Concho: A metal disk through which two slits have been cut. Lace or fabric is passed through the slits to secure it to a garment.

Feathers used in a bustle

Deer toe: The two hoof projections removed from the tips of the legs of the white-tailed deer. Used as sound-making, decorative elements on many pieces of dance regalia.

Dentalium: The shell of a saltwater mollusk found only in Puget Sound. Up to three centimeters in length, tubular, and off-white in color, the rare shell is a highly valued trade item. Dentalia are often incorporated into chokers, bracelets, and earrings.

Feather: Actually modified scales, feathers are a highly specialized, hollow-shafted covering for birds. Native Americans hold birds in high regard for their ability to fly and for their status as a "two-legged" creature. Feathers are used for bustles, headdresses, fans, and numerous other regalia items. Eagle and hawk feathers are particularly prized and are usually acquired as gifts of merit.

Jingles or cones used on the back of Jingle Dress Dance Regalia

Leather, especially deer hide, is used for leggings and moccasins

Ribbon fringe

Hide: The skin of an animal that must be treated (or "tanned") by natural or chemical processes before serving as a material for regalia. Deer, elk, and moose hide are the most commonly used hides in regalia making.

Jingle or Cone: A snuff or tobacco tin lid cut and twisted to form a cone shape. While used on many pieces of regalia, it is the primary decorative element of the Jingle Dress Dance regalia. The tinkly sound of jingles clinking against each other is an important feature of this dance.

Leather: A tanned hide; in the context of dance regalia, usually deer hide.

Megis shell: More commonly known as a cowrie shell, the megis shell is sometimes incorporated into regalia; quite often it is sewn on dresses or worn on neckties. Like the eagle feather, this small shell is an important symbol of a creation story. Through this shell the Creator blows life from the elements of the natural world into man.

Quill or Porcupine quill: The sharp-tipped, hollow, modified hair of the porcupine. They are used in their natural round shape on birch-bark boxes or in jewelry. When used instead of beadwork on clothing, they are soaked, flattened, and usually dyed. See Quillwork.

Ribbon fringe: A row of many ribbons, sometimes braided at the top, used to decorate the hems of shirts, dresses, and skirts.

Sequins: Brightly colored, reflective, commercially produced small plastic disks used in lieu of beads. Often used on Fancy Shawl Dance regalia.

Sinew: In a regalia context, this term originally referred to the tendons of game animals used as binding or lacing. Today it refers to a commercially produced, man-made synthetic.

Skin: Generally interchangeable with the term "pelt," a skin is the treated covering of a fur-bearing animal such as a beaver or coyote. Skins are used in a variety of ways in regalia manufacture.

Sweetgrass: A wild grass that thrives in low, wetland areas of the Great Lakes. Its name in the Anishinaabeg language is *weengush;* its Latin name is *Hierochloe odorata.* Sweetgrass is one of the four sacred plants of the Anishinaabe and is used for a variety of purposes. A three-stranded braid of sweetgrass, symbolizing the mind, body, and spirit, is often carried by dancers. This braid is referred to as the hair of *O'gushnan* (Our Mother the Earth).

Tobacco: *Samah* in Anishinaabem, tobacco is one of the four sacred plants. It is used as a gift of reciprocity or thanks and is often offered as a gift when asking an elder for help or instruction.

Trade silver: Silver items, including crosses, medals, gorgets, and broaches, historically traded to Native Americans during the fur-trade era. Sometimes also called German silver, it is actually a nickel/silver alloy. In addition to using original pieces intact, Native Americans rework trade silver and coins into other decorative pieces.

Trade wool or Stroud: A light, closely woven wool fabric. Stroud and heavier wool fabrics were often traded in the form of blankets and worn whole or resewn into a variety of clothing.

Yarn: Long strands of twisted threads of cotton, wool, or other material.

TECHNIQUES

Appliqué: Decoration made by sewing cut pieces of fabric or other materials onto supporting materials of often contrasting colors.

Beadwork decorates a heart-shaped purse

Beadwork: Beadwork can refer to nearly any type of handicraft, or portion of handicraft, which uses beads as a predominant material; it also refers to the process of constructing beads into these completed products. Beadwork usually consists of threading beads onto a string, then sewing the beads (either singly or in groups) in a line onto another, supportive material. The technique can be used to create linear patterns or solid areas of colored designs. Beadwork can also be done on a narrow loom; the resulting strip can be used as a choker, wrist band, hat band, or sewn onto another fabric as a decorative element.

Finger weaving: A simple weaving method used to produce narrow items such as sashes, garters, and bags.

Fringe work: An edging of leather strips, yarn, or ribbon used on some regalia items. Now a decoration, it once had a practical application as a means of shedding rain.

Quillwork: Term used to describe both a process and product. Porcupine quills are plucked, washed, sorted, sometimes dyed, and then affixed, either flattened or unflattened, onto a backing or supportive material. Like beads, quills can be used to create linear or solid designs. Quillwork is sometimes referred to as porcupine quill embroidery because the sharp quill must be pushed, like a needle and thread, through the backing material. The resulting patterns, like embroidered ones, are often very detailed and colorful.

Reverse appliqué: The process of creating a design by cutting away one layer of fabric to expose a bottom layer of fabric of contrasting color. The cut edges of the design on the top layer are usually turned under and sewn to the bottom layer.

Ribbonwork: A form of reverse-appliqué that uses ribbon or fabric cut in long strips. In Woodlands-style textiles, ribbonwork often incorporates mirror-image floral designs done in contrasting colors.

Tanning: The preparation of animal skin before it can be used as material for making regalia or other objects. The traditional Native American tanning method uses only natural materials (such as animal brains, ash, and salt). When used on deer skin, this process results in buckskin leather, which is soft to the touch and has a slightly textured surface. Commercial tanning, on the other hand, uses man-made chemicals and results in a stiffer, more smoothly finished leather. Both processes result in a white-colored leather; a cream or tan color can be achieved by smoking the hide or dyeing it with chemical products.

OTHER TERMINOLOGY

Anishnabe, Anishnaabek, Anishnabeg: A person of Native American (Indian) descent originally from the Great Lakes region. Differences in spelling are due to regional or tribal colloquial differences.

Anishinaabem: The language of the Anishinaabe people. The slang expression "speaking Indian" is sometimes heard.

Midé: A member of the Midewewin (Grand Medicine Society).

Pan-Indian: The movement in which specific and characteristic traits of a tribal group are incorporated into a more homogeneous Indian culture.

SUGGESTED READING

Benton-Banai, Edward. *The Mishomis Book: The Voice of the Ojibway.* St. Paul, Minnesota: Red School House, 1988.

Blackbird, Chief Andrew J. *History of the Ottawa and Chippewa Indians of Michigan.* Harbor Springs, Michigan, 1897.

Brown, Vanessa, and Barre Toelken. "American Indian Powwow." In *Folklife Annual 1987*, 46-69. Washington, D.C.: American Folklife Center, Library of Congress, 1987.

Cleland, Charles E. *Rites of Conquest: The History and Culture of Michigan's Native Americans.* Ann Arbor, Michigan: University of Michigan Press, 1992.

Clifton, James A., George L. Cornell, and James M. McClurken. *People of the Three Fires: The Ottawa, Potawatomi, and Ojibway of Michigan.* Grand Rapids, Michigan: The Michigan Indian Press, Grand Rapids Inter-Tribal Council, 1988.

Cronk, Michael Sam, with Beverly Cavanaugh and Franziska von Rosen. "Celebration: Native Events in Eastern Canada." In *Folklife Annual 1987*, 70-85. Washington, D.C.: American Folklife Center, Library of Congress, 1987.

Danzinger, Edmund Jefferson, Jr. *The Chippewas of Lake Superior.* Norman, Oklahoma: The University of Oklahoma Press, 1979.

Densmore, Frances. *Chippewa Customs.* Minneapolis, Minnesota: Minnesota Historical Society, 1979. [First printed in 1929 by the Smithsonian Institution Bureau of Ethnology as Bulletin 86.]

Flint Institute of Arts. *Art of the Great Lakes Indians.* Flint, Michigan: Flint Institute of Arts, 1973.

Garcia, Louis. "Short History of the Jingle Dress." *Whispering Wind Magazine* 5, no. 2 (1991): 21.

Harbor Springs Historical Commission. *Beadwork and Textiles of the Ottawa.* Harbor Springs, Michigan: Harbor Springs Historical Commission, 1984.

Harbor Springs Historical Commission. *Ottawa Quillwork on Birchbark.* Harbor Springs, Michigan: Harbor Springs Historical Commission, 1983.

Hartman, Sheryl. *Indian Clothing of the Great Lakes: 1740-1840.* Ogden, Utah: Eagle's View Publishing Company, 1988.

Heth, Charlotte. "Native American Dance: Ceremonies and Social Traditions." In *Native American Dance: Ceremonies and Social Traditions,* edited by Charlotte Heth, 1-18. Washington, D.C.: Smithsonian Institution National Museum of the American Indian with Starwood/Fulcrum Publishing, Inc., 1992.

Howard, James H. "Northern Style Grass Dance Costume." *American Indian Hobbyist* 7 (1960): 18-27.

_____. "Notes on the Dakota Grass Dance." *Southwest Journal of Anthropology* 8 (1951): 82-85.

Kelley, Helen. *Scarlet Ribbons: American Indian Technique for Today's Quilters.* Paducah, Kentucky: American Quilter's Society, 1987.

Kurath, Gertrude Prokosch. *Michigan Indian Festivals.* Ann Arbor, Michigan: Ann Arbor Publishers, 1966.

Lyford, Carrie A. *Ojibwa Crafts.* Stevens Point, Wisconsin: R. Schneider Publishers, 1982.

MacDowell, Marsha, ed. *Anishnaabek: Artists of Little Traverse Bay.* East Lansing, Michigan: Michigan State University Museum in collaboration with the Little Traverse Bay Bands of Odawa, 1996.

MacDowell, Marsha, and Jan Reed, eds. *Sisters of the Great Lakes: Art of American Indian Women.* East Lansing, Michigan: Michigan State University Museum in collaboration with the Nokomis Learning Center, 1996.

Monture, Joel. *The Complete Guide to Traditional Native American Beadwork.* New York: MacMillan General Reference, 1993.

Orchard, William C. *The Technique of Porcupine Quill Decoration Among the Indians of North America.* Liberty, Utah: Eagles View Publishing, 1984.

Paterek, Josephine. *Encyclopedia of American Indian Costume.* New York: W. W. Norton & Company, 1994.

Penney, David W. *Art of the American Frontier: The Chandler-Pohrt Collection.* Seattle, Washington: The University of Washington Press in association with the Detroit Institute of Arts, 1992.

Pfaff, Tim. *Paths of the People: The Ojibwe in the Chippewa Valley.* Eau Claire, Wisconsin: Chippewa Valley Museum Press, 1993.

Phillips, Ruth B. *Patterns of Power/Vers la force spirituelle: The Jasper Grant Collection and Great Lakes Indian Art of the Early Nineteenth Century.* Kleinburg, Ontario: The McMichael Canadian Collection, 1985.

Plains Art Museum. *On the Border: Native American Weaving Traditions of the Great Lakes and Prairie.* Moorhead, Minnesota: Plains Art Museum, 1990.

Powers, William K. *"Feathers" Costume.* Kendall Park, New Jersey: Lakota Books, 1994.

_____. *Grass Dance Costume.* Kendall Park, New Jersey: Lakota Books, 1994.

_____. "Innovation in Lakota Pow Wow Costumes." *American Indian Art Magazine* 19, no. 4 (Autumn 1994): 66-73.

Quimby, George Irving. *Indian Culture and European Trade Goods.* Milwaukee, Wisconsin: University of Wisconsin, 1966.

Ritzenhaler, Robert W., and Pat Ritzenhaler. *The Woodland Indians of the Western Great Lakes.* Garden City, New York: The Natural History Press, American Museum Science Books for The American Museum of Natural History, 1969.

Roberts, Chris. *Pow Wow Country.* Helena, Montana: American and World Geographic Publishing, 1992.

Sault Ste. Marie Tribe of Chippewa Indians. *O'gushnann (Our Mother): A Collection of Writings by and about Anishnabe of the Eastern Upper Peninsula of Michigan.* Sault Ste. Marie, Michigan: Sault Ste. Marie Tribe of Chippewa Indians, 1982.

Smith, Theresa S. *The Island of the Anishnaabeg.* Moscow, Idaho: University of Idaho Press, 1995.

Smithsonian Institution. *Naamikaaged: Dancer for the People.* Washington, D.C.: Smithsonian Folkways, 1996.

Vennum, Thomas. *The Ojibway Dance Drum.* Smithsonian Folklife Studies, no. 2. Washington, D.C.: Smithsonian Institution, 1982.

SUGGESTED VIEWING

"Into the Circle: An Introduction to Native American Pow Wows." Tulsa, Oklahoma: Full Circle Communications, 1992. Video.

"Native American Men's and Women's Dance Styles, Volume 1." Tulsa, Oklahoma: Full Circle Communications, 1993. Video.

"Wisconsin Pow Wow/Naamikaaged: Dancer for the People." Washington, D.C.: Smithsonian Institution, 1996. Two-video set with 40-page booklet.

Chi Noden Drum. Michigan State University American Indian Heritage Pow Wow, 1995.

CONTRIBUTORS

THURMAN BEAR/MKOONS ("Little Bear") (Ojibwa) was born in Rhinelander, Wisconsin, in 1943. In 1966, after serving in the military, he settled in Detroit, where he works at American Indian Health and Family Services of Southeastern Michigan. Bear remembers attending pow wows with his parents in Oklahoma in the early 1950s. As a Fancy Dancer, he was a regular participant in Michigan's early contemporary pow wows. Today Bear is recognized as an accomplished bustle maker and a knowledgeable and entertaining pow wow master of ceremonies, or "Emcee."

MARCLAY CRAMPTON (Saginaw Chippewa/Grand River Ottawa) is educational coordinator for the Nokomis Learning Center. In addition to being a talented craftsperson, Crampton is a member of the board of directors of the Ziibiwing Cultural Society, located at the Saginaw Chippewa Indian Tribe Reservation. Members of Crampton's family were deeply involved in the establishment of the Hastings pow wows.

JASON GEORGE/DE WAH HE DOKE ("MOON CUT IN HALF") (Oneida/Ojibwa/Potawatomi) was born in Sarnia, Ontario, in 1967 and grew up on the Kettle Point Reserve in Ontario. He started fancy dancing at age 13 and has since placed in numerous regional competition pow wows. George acquired his regalia-making skills from several different people: he learned beadwork, appliqué, and sewing from his parents and bustle making from members of the Klein family. George resides in Lansing, where he attends college and sings in the High Spirit Drum.

CATHERINE GIBSON/OZAWAUM BENESHEE ("YELLOW BIRD WOMAN") (Odawa) was born in 1959. She first learned beadwork from family and friends when she was about nine years old. She estimates that she has made or worked on more than 50 sets of dance regalia, and her excellent work is much in demand. Gibson (née Shananaquet) lives in the Petoskey area with her husband and their two children.

CHARLOTTE HETH (Cherokee) is head of public programs, National Museum of the American Indian, Smithsonian Institution. She is the general editor of *Native American Dance: Ceremonies and Social Traditions*. She has also served as director of the American Indian Studies Program at the University of California at Los Angeles, where she received a doctorate in music.

NETAWN ALICE KIOGIMA (Odawa/Ojibwa/Blackfoot) began dancing in 1991 and now regularly attends pow wows throughout the country. She was elected Miss Odawa Homecoming in 1992. Kiogima works at the Ziibiwing Cultural Center, a cultural resource center of the Saginaw Chippewa Indian tribe. She is pursuing a college degree and plans to become a certified teacher in the Native American community.

MARSHA MACDOWELL is a professor of art at Michigan State University and curator of folk arts at the Michigan State University Museum. She coordinates the Michigan Traditional Arts Program, a partnership between the museum and the Michigan Council for Arts and Cultural Affairs. She serves on the MSU American Indian Heritage Pow Wow committee and has collaborated with Native Americans on a variety of research, documentation, and exhibition projects related to traditional expressive arts.

ANTHONY "TONY" MIRON (Ojibwa), a member of the Sault Ste. Marie Tribe of Chippewa Indians, lives in Mikado, a historical community of Native Americans in Michigan's lower peninsula. Miron is a multitalented artist who works in many media, including drawing, woodcarving, and painting. In addition to dancing on the pow wow circuit from Ontario to Oklahoma, he frequently makes educational presentations on dance and dance regalia.

ELIZABETH OSAWAMICK/GINIW MIIGWAN ("GOLDEN EAGLE FEATHER") (Ojibway) was born in 1967 in Little Current, Ontario, and currently lives in Peterborough, Ontario. Although she started dancing as a Women's Traditional Dancer at the age of 7, she did not dance for many years until 1993, when she returned to the dance arena as a Jingle Dress Dancer. She credits her cousins and aunts as major influences on her dancing.

ARNIE PARISH (Bay Mills Ojibway) has extensive pow wow experience as an Emcee, dancer, and singer. He is completing a doctoral degree in education at Michigan State University, where he works as a specialist at the MSU Native American Institute. He is also a researcher and consultant on many issues pertaining to Native American education at the state and tribal levels. He also serves on the MSU American Indian Heritage Pow Wow committee.

JUDITH PIERZYNOWSKI (Odawa/Chippewa), a member of the Little Traverse Bay Band of Odawa, was born in 1960 to the King family of Cross Village, Michigan. Pierzynowski has lived in the East Lansing area for the past 15 years and works for Michigan State University as a groundskeeper. She learned to make regalia from her relatives and her own trial-and-error experience. She frequents pow wows throughout Michigan and enjoys dancing and socializing with friends and family.

STANLEY PELTIER (Odawa), a member of the Odawa Nation of Wowashkesh (Deer Clan), was born in 1946 in Wikwemikong on Manitoulin Island, Ontario, where he still resides. Like many older members of this very close-knit and traditional community, Peltier was raised in a household that spoke Anishinaabem (the Anishinaabe language). Peltier began dancing in his teens and continues to be active in pow wows around the Great Lakes region.

DENNIS SHANANAQUET (Odawa) was born in 1963 in the Petoskey area and now resides with his family in Walloon Lake, Michigan. An accomplished pow wow dancer, he is also a talented industrial shop worker. Shananaquet sings with the "Skin Tones" drum, which plays at numerous pow wows throughout the state and is frequently requested as a host drum.

SALLY THIELEN/MASHUE ("SOUTH EAGLE WOMAN") (Chippewa) was born and raised in Sanford and now lives in Davison, Michigan. Though she worked for years as a nurse, she is now a full-time artist who explores the richness of her cultural heritage. Thielen works primarily in beadwork, clay, and her own handmade papers. Her porcelain masks, cast from Native American friends, family members, and acquaintances, have been exhibited extensively throughout the United States, Canada, Europe, Japan, and Africa.

FRANCES VINCENT is manager of the Michigan Traditional Arts Traveling Exhibits Program at the Michigan State University Museum. A former exhibit designer for The South Bank Centre (London) and the anthropology galleries of the Cambridge University Museum of Archaeology and Anthropology, Vincent has recently served as designer for several exhibits related to Native American culture, including "Sisters of the Great Lakes: Art of American Indian Women" and "Anishnaabek: Artists of Little Traverse Bay."

MINNIE WABANIMKEE (Odawa), is a freelance photojournalist. Born in northern Michigan, she currently resides in Cedar with her daughter, Kelsey. Wabanimkee has received numerous awards, including the Robert F. Kennedy Journalism Award for Excellence in Photo Journalism. She has worked for the Associated Press, the Michigan State University Museum, the Nokomis Learning Center, and several tribes within the state. Her most recent work is included in the Michigan State University Museum exhibit and publication "Anishnaabek: Artists of Little Traverse Bay."

BEDAHBIN WEBKAMIGAD (Odawa/Ojibwa/Potawatomi) was born 1972 in Low Current, Ontario, and lives in East Lansing with her husband Tony Bardy and their two children, Zhaawoshkogiizhik and Waawaaskonenhs. Webkamigad has danced in pow wows all her life. She began making regalia in her childhood and now regularly makes items for friends and family. In addition to working as a consultant to the Michigan State University Museum, she has been active with the Lansing North American Indian Center and the Michigan State University Native American Indian Student Organization.

CAMERON WOOD is director of the Nokomis Learning Center. He has worked as an intern and staff member of several museums, including the Wheelwright Museum of the American Indian (Santa

Fe, New Mexico), the R. E. Olds Transportation Museum (Lansing, Michigan), and the Michigan State University Museum.

LINDA TOPASH YAZEL/MUSKO BAHNASE ("RED BIRD") (Potawatomi/Ojibway) resides in Buchanan, Michigan, with her husband. Although as a child she did not have the opportunity to participate in the arts of her tribal heritage, she has spent the last two decades of her life learning and honing traditional skills. Yazel beads with her aunts and cousins and is well known for her intricate beadwork, especially her detailed loom beading. She teaches beading at galleries and museums, regularly attends pow wows in the region, and serves on a local pow wow committee.

Above: Men's Traditional Dancer (right). Annual Homecoming of the Three Fires Pow Wow, Grand Rapids, 1996.

Left: Men's Traditional Dancer among the crowd. Sault Ste. Marie Tribal National Assembly, 14th Annual Traditional Pow Wow and Spiritual Conference, 1996.

Below: Dancers under the arbor. Sault Ste. Marie Tribal National Assembly, 14th Annual Traditional Pow Wow and Spiritual Conference, 1996.

*Unidentified dancer. Michigan State
University American Indian Heritage
Pow Wow, East Lansing, 1996.*

The exhibit "Contemporary Great Lakes Pow Wow Regalia: *Nda Maamawigaami* (Together We Dance)" opened at the Nokomis Learning Center, Okemos, Michigan, in March 1997.

The Nokomis Learning Center, located in Okemos, Michigan, is a nonprofit organization dedicated to the preservation and presentation of the culture and tradition of the People of the Three Fires (Ottawa, Potawatomi, and Ojibwa). It offers exhibitions, educational programs, special events, and publications. For more information, please call 517/349-5777.

The Michigan State University Museum was founded in 1857 and is one of the state's most popular natural and cultural history museums. The Michigan Traditional Arts Program (MTAP) at the Michigan State University Museum advances cultural understanding and equity in a diverse society through the documentation, preservation, and presentation of the state's folk arts and folklife. For information about museum tours, classes, public programs, exhibitions, the Michigan State University Museum Associates, and MTAP programs and services, please call 517/355-2370.

Editing, design, and production supervision:
Division of University Relations, Michigan State University
Kristan Tetens, publication project manager
Cynthia Lounsbery, publication design manager

Color separation, printing, and binding:
Lawson Printers, Battle Creek, Michigan